Do you know about Animals?

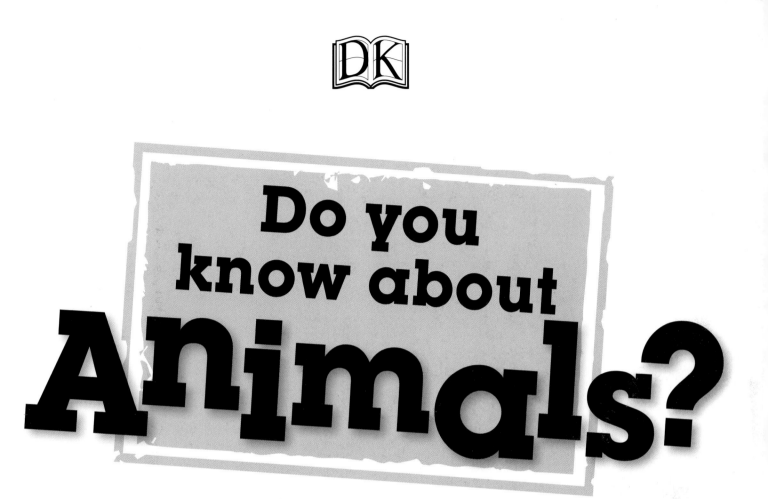

Do you know about Animals?

Derek Harvey

Penguin Random House

Author Derek Harvey

DK LONDON
Project editor Sam Priddy
Designer Lucy Sims
Editors Katy Lennon, Olivia Stanford
Additional design Emma Hobson
Managing editor Laura Gilbert
Managing art editor Diane Peyton Jones
Pre-production producer Nikoleta Parasaki
Producer Srijana Gurung
Art director Martin Wilson
Publisher Sarah Larter
Publishing director Sophie Mitchell

DK DELHI
Project editor Suneha Dutta
Editor Ishani Nandi
Assistant art editor Kartik Gera
Art editor Nehal Verma
Senior editor Shatarupa Chaudhuri
Senior art editor Nishesh Batnagar
Managing editor Alka Thakur Hazarika
Managing art editor Romi Chakraborty
DTP designers Bimlesh Tiwary, Syed Md Farhan
CTS manager Balwant Singh
Production manager Pankaj Sharma
Senior picture researcher Sumedha Chopra

First published in Great Britain in 2016 by
Dorling Kindersley Limited
80 Strand, London, WC2R 0RL

A CIP catalogue record for this book
is available from the British Library.
ISBN: 978-0-2412-2815-9

Printed and bound in China

A WORLD OF IDEAS:
SEE ALL THERE IS TO KNOW

www.dk.com

Contents

Mammals

Birds

Underwater

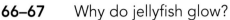

Creepy-crawlies

Reptiles and amphibians

Discover which colours I can see on pages 34–35.

Find out how I walk up walls on pages 114–115.

Mammals

Mammals are warm-blooded animals that are usually covered in fur. All mammal mums produce milk to feed their babies.

Nose
Wolves can pick up a prey's scent trail from up to 2.4 km (1.5 miles) away.

Pack leader
A dominant (alpha) male guides the pack and takes control of hunts.

Why do wolves live in packs?

A wolf is a skilful predator. It has sharp teeth, a strong bite, and is incredibly cunning. But it has another deadly weapon: teamwork. Wolves work together in packs to hunt down large prey.

? *Quick quiz*

1. How many wolves are in a wolf pack?

2. What happens when two packs meet?

3. Why do wolves howl at the sky?

See pages 134–135 for the answers

Expressions
Wolves use facial expressions, along with scent and sounds, to communicate with other members in the pack.

Wolves can take down prey as large as an elk.

Which other animals hunt together?

Lions
Most cats hunt alone, but female lions work in a team. Together, they stalk their prey from all sides – so when it finally bolts there is a good chance it will run straight into one of them. The other lions then help to bring down the kill, before taking it back to the family.

Humpback whales
Groups of humpback whales circle beneath shoals of tiny fish and create a bubble "net" to herd them tightly together. The whales then swim upwards at great speed to gobble down massive mouthfuls of fish in one fell swoop.

Why do tigers have stripes?

Many tigers have golden fur and thin black stripes to blend into long, dry grass. Being well camouflaged against their surroundings means tigers can get very close to their target without being seen – so a quick pounce is all that's needed to catch dinner.

Can you spot these hidden animals?

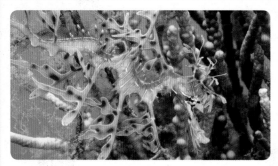

Leafy seadragon
This fish, a relative of seahorses, has leaf-like fins so that it is perfectly camouflaged among seaweed.

Leaf-tailed gecko
This lizard's skin matches the appearance of bark. By lying still on a branch it can catch unsuspecting insects.

Flashing ears

As well as black stripes on their bodies, some tigers also have white dots on the back of their ears. These may help cubs follow their mum through the grass.

Vertical stripes

Black stripes help to break up the outline of the tiger's body. This fools prey, even when the tiger is really close to it.

Golden colour

Most tigers have orange fur, which matches the golden colour of the grass and the fallen leaf litter in the forest.

? Quick quiz

1. What does "camouflage" mean?

2. Which other cats have stripes?

3. Why do zebras have stripes?

See pages 134–135 for the answers

More than half of the 900 known species of bat use echolocation when they are in flight.

Moth
Bats hunt all kinds of flying insects – but fat moths provide particularly big meals.

How do bats find food in the dark?

Bats fly at night and most have a taste for fluttering insects. But how can you find dinner in the air when you can't see it, smell it, or hear it? The trick is to make a clicking noise, and listen for the echo that bounces back from the tiny prey. This is called echolocation.

? Quick quiz

1. Can bats see?

2. How do bats produce their clicks?

3. Do all bats feed on insects?

See pages 134–135 for the answers

How echolocation works

The call of a bat is so high-pitched that humans can't hear it. But a bat's ears are tuned into the echoes coming back from flying insects – or obstacles in their way.

The bat's clicking noise

Echo coming back from the moth

Ears

Bats have big ears to help pick up the sounds of their echoing clicks.

Tail trap

Once an insect is caught in the bat's mouth, its legs scoop its tail forward to help stop the insect escaping.

Can any other animals use echolocation?

Dolphins

A dolphin makes whistles and clicks in air sacs under its blowhole. The sounds help dolphins communicate with one another, but are also used for echolocation in murky waters. Dolphins listen for clicks echoing back from tasty fish.

Oilbirds

Oilbirds spend the day sleeping in caves, but use echolocation when they wake up in the evening. The echoes of their clicks in the darkness help prevent midair collisions with other oilbirds, before they emerge from the cave to eat fruit.

What is a tusk?

Imagine having teeth that keep on growing, even when they've extended out of your mouth. Walrus tusks are extra-large canine teeth that grow downwards from the upper jaw, then curve backwards. Like elephant tusks, they are made of a hard substance called ivory.

Are all tusks the same shape?

Babirusa
Some pigs have tusks that grow upwards from the lower jaw. They are especially curly in tropical pigs called babirusas.

Narwhal
Most animal tusks are curved and come in pairs, but narwhals (relatives of dolphins) have single straight ones.

An elephant's tusk is the largest tooth of any living animal.

Show-off

Bigger walruses bully smaller ones to get the best resting spots by leaning backwards to really show off their tusks.

Whiskers

Walruses don't use their tusks to dig for food, but snuffle in the mud for clams using their sensitive whiskers.

Tusks

Walruses use their tusks for cutting holes in the ice to breathe through, or to hang off icy ledges while snoozing in the water.

? Quick quiz

1. Where do walruses live in the wild?

2. Why do walruses have such thick skin?

3. Why do male walruses have bigger tusks than females?

See pages 134–135 for the answers

Do giraffes get dizzy when they bend over?

When a human quickly bends over and stands back up they might get dizzy because of a sudden rush of blood to and from the brain. Because giraffes grow as tall as houses they have special blood vessels in their necks to stop this from happening.

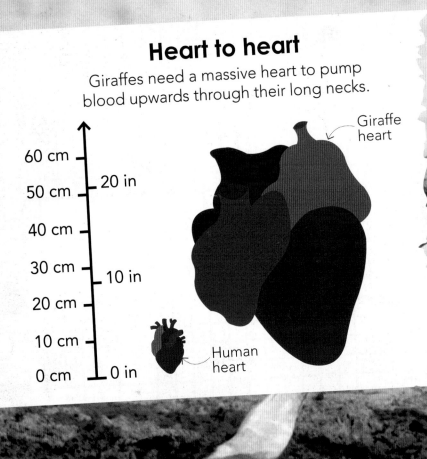

Heart to heart

Giraffes need a massive heart to pump blood upwards through their long necks.

Giraffe heart

Human heart

60 cm
50 cm — 20 in
40 cm
30 cm — 10 in
20 cm
10 cm
0 cm — 0 in

A giraffe can grow to 6 m (19 ft 8 in) tall, making it the tallest land animal alive.

? Picture quiz

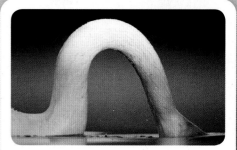

Which long-necked animal is this?

See pages 134–135 for the answer

Long neck

When the giraffe's head is down, special valves in its blood vessels snap shut to stop blood rushing downwards too quickly and flooding the brain.

Back of the head

A net of tiny tubes at the base of a giraffe's skull act like a sponge to reduce the extra flow of blood when its head is down.

Long legs

A giraffe's legs are so long that it has to stretch them outwards in order for its head to reach the ground to drink.

Why do some animals have long necks?

Gerenuk

This African gazelle reaches leaves by stretching its long neck and even standing up on its back legs.

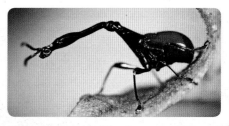

Giraffe-necked weevil

Male giraffe-necked weevils use their long necks to fight each other when competing for mates.

Do mammals lay eggs?

Most mammal mums give birth to live young, but the platypus and echidna from Australia lay eggs instead. Mammals that lay eggs are called monotremes. They keep their eggs warm until they hatch into blind, hairless babies. The mother then feeds them on milk, just like other mammals.

Duck-like bill

The platypus has a rubbery bill for scooping up worms and shrimp to eat. Females need this food in order to have enough energy to produce milk for feeding their young.

Comparing eggs

Platypus eggs are often less than half the size of the average chicken egg. They hatch approximately ten days after they are laid.

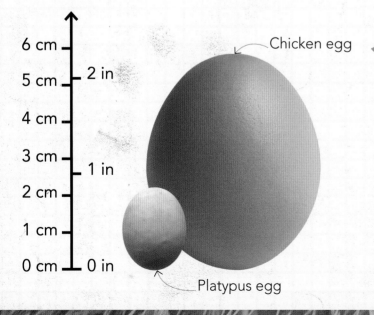

6 cm
5 cm — 2 in
4 cm
3 cm — 1 in
2 cm
1 cm
0 cm — 0 in

Chicken egg

Platypus egg

Limbs

The platypus has webbed feet to help it swim through water. Males have a poisonous spike on their heel, which they use for self-defence and to compete for mates.

How do other mammals look after their young?

Marsupials

Most marsupials keep their young in pouches. Marsupial babies are tiny when they are born: a new-born kangaroo is no bigger than a peanut. Babies stay in their mother's pouches and drink her milk to grow strong.

Placentals

Placentals, such as these pigs, are mammals that keep babies in their womb so they can grow bigger before birth. Mums develop a placenta – a special organ that provides food for the baby while it is in her womb.

? Picture **quiz**

Is a cat a monotreme, a marsupial, or a placental?

See pages 134–135 for the answer

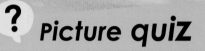

Soft fur

Short, waterproof fur keeps the platypus and its egg warm in its bankside burrow.

Blood vessels

Elephant ears contain lots of blood vessels. Warm blood flows through them and heat escapes from the ear's surface.

Trunk

An elephant's trunk is its most important tool. It is used for smelling, touching, and breathing – as well as squirting water over itself to keep cool.

Ears

Elephants use their ears a bit like fans. Flapping them helps to cool them down.

How do other animals cool down?

Indian rhinoceros

There's nothing like rolling around in cool mud. Big thick-skinned mammals, such as this rhinoceros, find it a good way to escape the heat of the day.

Shovel-snouted lizard

This African lizard performs acrobatics to stop its toes from burning on the sun-scorched sand. It lifts its feet alternately, so each foot touches the surface for just a short time.

See pages 134–135 for the answers

? Quick quiz

1. Where do elephants live in the wild?

2. How long do elephants live for?

3. What is an elephant "matriarch"?

Why do elephants have big ears?

As the biggest land animal, elephants can get incredibly hot living under the tropical sun. The African elephant's enormous ears help it to lose some of the heat that is generated by its massive body.

What's in a camel's hump?

Camels have special features for surviving in the desert. You could travel a long way before you find food or water, but this doesn't bother a camel. Its humps contain enough fat to keep it alive for up to three weeks. Water is no problem either. When it gets a chance, a camel can guzzle down a bathful in ten minutes.

Who can survive the longest without food?

Crocodiles
Crocodiles can gulp down huge prey – even digesting bones, horns, and hooves. A big meal like this can keep them going for months before they have to kill again.

Olms
This strange white salamander inhabits cold, dark cave waters in Europe. It can go without food for years and has a lifespan of 100 years or more.

Eyelashes
Sandstorms are common in the desert, so camels have long eyelashes to stop sand from getting in their eyes.

Nostrils
To prevent sand going up their noses, camels can close their nostrils!

Each hump contains up to 35 kg (77 lb) of fat.

Floppy humps

If the camel stops eating it starts to use the fat stored in its humps, which then go floppy! When it has another meal, the fatty humps build up again.

Normal humps   Floppy humps

Humps

Bactrian camels have two humps, while dromedary camels only have one.

? True or false?

1. Camels get water from their humps.

2. Lots of camels live in Australia.

3. Camels defend themselves by spitting.

See pages 134–135 for the answers

Can porcupines shoot their spines?

Porcupines cannot shoot their spines, but they don't really need to. An angry porcupine charging backwards can put off the hungriest of predators. As well as this, their long spines can break off to lodge in the flesh of any animal that gets too close.

? Picture quiz

Which animal has had a run-in with a porcupine?

See pages 134–135 for the answer

Wary lion
Even a big predator, like a lion, is careful around a prickly porcupine. Just a single spine gives a painful jab.

What other animals have defence tactics?

Skunk

Skunks have black and white markings that warn predators to stay away from them. If an approaching animal is not careful it may get a nasty surprise. If threatened, a skunk will do a head-stand and squirt a stinking fluid from glands near its bottom. It can aim for the eyes to blind an attacker.

Armadillo

An armadillo has no way of fighting opponents if it is attacked. Instead, it has bony plates under its skin, which form a shield over its back and head. An armadillo can even roll up into a tight ball so that even its soft belly is protected by its armour.

Porcupine spines can kill! A lion can die from an infected spine injury.

Puffed up

A porcupine can raise its spines just like many mammals can raise their hair. It makes it look bigger and scarier to an approaching predator.

Alarming tail

A porcupine's tail spines are hollow, so when it shakes its tail it makes a loud rattling warning sound.

Grasping tail

A spider monkey's tail is prehensile, meaning it is used for grasping. It even has a palm-like patch of bare skin for getting a better grip.

Spider monkeys get their name from their spider-like limbs and tail.

How do monkeys swing through the trees?

Monkeys use their grasping hands and feet for climbing – but not all have the extra-special skills for swinging through the branches. Some South American monkeys, like the spider monkey, can do it with the help of their gripping tail. The tail works like a fifth limb, helping the hanging monkey swing across big gaps between the high branches.

Long arms

Spider monkeys have long arms for hanging from the branches. This makes them more acrobatic than many other monkeys.

Long fingers

Spider monkeys have long fingers for hooking over branches. Each foot has a big toe that can also grip.

? Quick quiz

1. Do all monkeys have a prehensile tail?

2. Who swings through the trees the fastest?

3. How can the hands or feet of monkeys grip so well?

See pages 134–135 for the answers

Which animals speed through the trees in a different way?

Gibbons

Gibbons, from Southeast Asia, are the king of the swingers. They use their hook-like hands and extra-strong arms to swing forwards under the branches.

Sifakas

This Madagascan lemur has strong legs for leaping from tree to tree, while gripping the trunks with its hands. It uses its tail to help it keep its balance.

Why do lions have sharp teeth?

Animals that eat mostly meat need teeth as sharp as knives. Lions have pointed teeth that can pierce the tough flesh of a large buffalo quickly and easily.

Canines

Lions suffocate their prey by clamping their front canine teeth around the victim's throat.

Back teeth

A lion's strong back teeth have sharp edges that work like blades to slice up prey.

Only male lions have a mane of hair.

Carnivore teeth

Carnivores (meat-eaters) have sharp teeth, as well as strong jaw muscles that enable them to attack with a fierce bite.

Herbivore teeth

Herbivores (plant-eaters) have flat-topped back teeth with sharp ridges to grind tough leaves.

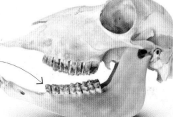

Rough tongue

A lion's tongue is covered in tiny hooks, which helps it to scrape meat from bones.

Do all carnivores have the same teeth?

Great white sharks

Each tooth of a great white shark has a jagged edge, so each one can slice and cut. Unlike mammals, sharks continually replace lost teeth. Their wide jaws have a strong bite, too.

Crocodiles

The pointed teeth of a crocodile are useful for stabbing, but not much good for slicing. Crocodiles snap their strong jaws and twist their entire body to pull prey apart.

? Picture quiz

Who do these teeth belong to?

See pages 134–135 for the answer

Why do meerkats stand on their back legs?

When you're the size of a squirrel and you live on the ground, you need to stand as tall as possible to keep an eye on what is happening around you. Meerkats stand on their back legs to spot distant danger, and occasionally to enjoy the sunshine!

Meerkats take it in turns to keep watch for one hour.

? Quick quiz

1. How do meerkats signal that danger is coming?

2. How do meerkats escape from danger?

3. Are all the meerkats in a group related?

See pages 134–135 for the answers

Back legs

Meerkats walk around on four legs. But they are good at balancing on their two hind legs as well.

Eyes

Meerkats have excellent vision for spotting predators. Adults keep watch over the group from a high rock and alert each other when they spot danger.

Heat patch

Meerkats have a patch of bare black skin on their chest that is really good for soaking up heat when they sunbathe.

Which other animals warn each other of danger?

Vervet monkeys

Vervet monkeys are high climbers and can spot faraway danger. They have different alarm calls for snakes, eagles, or leopards.

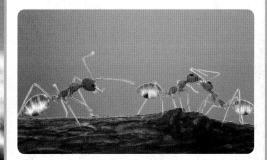

Weaver ants

When their nests are under attack, weaver ants release special chemicals, called pheromones, that warn the rest of the colony.

Are moles blind?

They might have tiny eyes, but moles aren't blind. They just can't see very well! However, if you spend your life in a pitch-black tunnel, a good sense of touch is much more useful, and moles are experts at feeling for worms.

The star-nosed mole has 25,000 touch sensors on its special nose.

Which animals really can't see?

Golden moles
The golden mole, from southern Africa, is not actually related to the dark-coloured moles. Its eyes are covered with skin so it can't see anything at all.

Mexican cave tetras
Over a million years ago some of these fish swam into underground cave waters. They've stayed in the darkness ever since, and have become blind by losing their eyes completely.

Small eye

A mole's eye is barely wider than 1 mm (0.04 in). It is probably sensitive to light, movement, and some colour, but it cannot see in much detail.

Digging claws

In complete darkness, moles use their big-clawed "hands" like shovels to dig through the soil.

Nosy sensors

The North American star-nosed mole has 22 wiggling tentacles on its snout that are extra sensitive for detecting tiny prey.

? Quick quiz

1. What is special about a mole's fur?

2. What are "mole hills"?

3. How much food does a mole eat each day?

See pages 134–135 for the answers

Can dogs see colour?

Our eyes contain different colour sensors, so we can see all the colours of a rainbow. But dogs have fewer kinds of colour sensors. Like us, they can see blue – but to them, red and green look like yellow.

Colours that humans see

Colours that dogs see

Quick quiz

1. Which animals have good colour vision?

2. Why are some people colour-blind?

See pages 134–135 for the answers

Dog vision

The dog sees the blue ball, but the other three coloured balls look similar to him: they all look yellowish.

Can animals sense things differently from humans?

Bees
Humans can't see ultraviolet light, but bees can. Ultraviolet patterns on flowers, like the dark marks on the image on the right, guide them to sources of nectar.

Snakes
Some snakes rely on special heat sensors on their head to find the warm bodies of prey, such as this dog.

Human vision

As well as the blue ball, the girl sees three more colours: yellow, green, and red.

Colour sensors

Human eyes have red, blue, and green sensors. The girl uses red and green ones together to see yellow (and red and blue ones together to see violet).

Do bears eat honey?

Even though bears are related to meat-eating cats and dogs, many also enjoy sweeter foods, like honey. Sun bears, from tropical Asia, are the smallest type of bear, and have the sweetest tooth of all. They can't resist raiding beehives for honey, and even angry bees won't put them off.

Beehive

Bees make honey from nectar, which they gather from flowers. They store honey in special cells inside a hive, and defend their supply by stinging intruders.

Sting-proof skin

In the hot tropics, thin fur keeps the bear cool. But its skin is extra thick to help stop bee stings.

? Quick quiz

1. Bears are omnivorous. What does this mean?

2. Which kind of bear eats more meat than any other?

3. Which bear eats bamboo?

See pages 134–135 for the answers

....Long tongue

The sun bear has the longest tongue of any bear. It is perfect for lapping up honey or getting into the nests of insects, such as termites.

Is it a myth?

Do monkeys eat bananas?

Some monkeys love fresh fruit, such as bananas. Like humans, they can see colour well, and look out for the colours that tell them fruit is ripe.

Do mice eat cheese?

Mice would have to be very hungry to eat cheese, and they stay away from the smelliest kinds. They prefer grain, but also like sweet things like biscuits.

....Long claws

A sun bear uses its powerful front limbs for climbing and its strong claws can easily rip open honey-filled hives.

Furry ears

A polar bear's hearing is extremely sensitive, especially to the sound of the bear's natural prey – such as seals.

Fatty skin

Many animals in cold places, including polar bears and penguins, have fat under their skin to help trap body heat inside.

Killer claws

The polar bear has hunter's claws – but also extra fur on the soles of its feet to help grip the slippery ice.

The polar bear is the world's biggest land carnivore (meat-eater).

Why don't polar bears eat penguins?

The Arctic and Antarctic are both covered in snow, but otherwise they really are poles apart. On the top of the world is the icy Arctic, where polar bears live. But at the bottom, freezing Antarctica has different kinds of animals, including penguins. Some penguins live a bit further north, but none ever cross into the northern half of the planet – so polar bears and penguins never meet.

What does eat penguins?

Leopard seals
Danger to penguins usually comes from the ocean. Leopard seals are especially fast in the water and prey on penguins.

Killer whales
A penguin is hardly a mouthful for a big killer whale – but that doesn't stop them when they fancy a snack!

Where they live

Polar bears live on land and floating ice in the Arctic. Twenty kinds of penguin live in the southern half of the planet – in places such as South America, Africa, Australasia, and Antarctica.

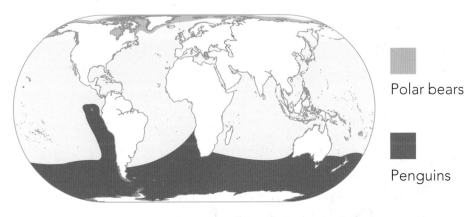

Polar bears

Penguins

? Quick quiz

1. Are there any land predators of penguins in Antarctica?

2. Which kind of penguin lives furthest north?

3. Do any flightless birds live in the Arctic?

See pages 134–135 for the answers

Birds

Birds are creatures that are covered in feathers. Most birds can fly, but there are a few, such as ostriches and penguins, that can't.

Why do ducks float?

Hollow bones and air pockets inside their bodies make ducks lighter than water. Oily feathers keep them waterproof, so their bodies don't become wet and heavy. This is why ducks always bob up to the surface and never sink.

Feathers
Feathers trap air, which helps ducks float.

Waterproof
A gland near the duck's tail produces oil. This coats the feathers, making them waterproof enough for droplets to simply roll off.

Paddling
On the surface of the water, ducks move forwards by kicking their webbed feet.

? Picture quiz

Which bird is so buoyant it needs to make a quick dive to catch fish before it pops up?

See pages 134–135 for the answer

Beak

Ducks use their beaks to spread the oil over their entire bodies to make them waterproof.

Some sea ducks can dive 60 m (196 ft) underwater, while most ducks can only dive 2 m (6 ft).

Air float

Like most birds, ducks have air sacs inside them, which are like balloons. They fill up with air, making the ducks lighter and helping them float.

Light bones

All flying birds, including waterbirds such as ducks, have hollow bones that make them lightweight. This helps ducks stay afloat.

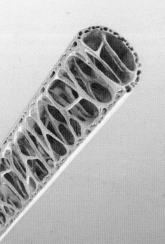

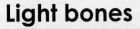

In what other ways do animals travel on water?

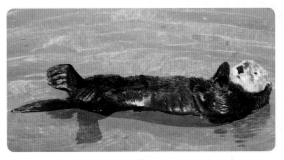

Floating

The sea otter has the densest fur coat of any animal, which traps a lot of warm air, helping it stay afloat. It can even sleep while floating on its back.

Sailing

The Portuguese man-of-war has a gas-filled bladder that it uses as a sail to float across the ocean's surface, while its tentacles dangle below.

Why are flamingos pink?

Flamingos get their colour from their food. These birds live near lakes filled with brine shrimps. Although flamingos' feathers are grey or white when they are born, eating the shrimps every day turns their feathers pink.

Colourful feathers

A flamingo's colour can range from pale pink to dark red and even bright orange. It all depends on how many shrimps they eat.

? Quick quiz

1. Why do flamingos need a special diet in zoos?

2. How is a baby flamingo's beak different to an adult's?

3. How many eggs does a female flamingo lay at a time?

See pages 134–135 for the answers

Brine shrimps

The pink colour of brine shrimps, in turn, comes from their diet of tiny plant-like living things called algae. Some flamingos feed directly on algae, which turns them even pinker.

The biggest flock of flamingos was estimated to contain over 2 million birds.

Beak

To eat, a flamingo dips its beak into the lake, then moves the water over rows of hairs in its mouth with its tongue to strain out the tiny shrimps.

Who else is coloured by food?

Ghost ants

These insects have see-through stomachs. Any food they eat, such as these coloured sugar-water droplets, can be seen from the outside.

Sea slugs

These soft-bodied sea creatures get many of their bright colours from grazing on corals and anemones.

Foot work

A flamingo uses its feet to pat the mud in the shallow waters of a lake to stir up the brine shrimps. Then it can scoop them up in its beak.

How do owls hunt at night?

Owls hunt in the dark using super-sensitive ears that can hear the faintest rustling sound made by animals, even from a distance. Once they have detected their prey, they silently swoop down from the sky to take it by surprise.

? Quick quiz

1. How do owls eat prey?
   a) With small, sharp teeth
   b) By swallowing it whole
   c) By tearing it into pieces

2. An owl can turn its head nearly full circle because…
   a) its eyes are too big to move
   b) it likes to stretch its neck
   c) its backbone is very short

See pages 134–135 for the answers

Silent wings
The soft, fluffy-edged feathers of an owl allow it to flap its wings without a "whooshing" sound that could alert the prey.

Clear sounds
The sound coming from the mouse may be faint to humans, but the owl can hear it very clearly.

Scurrying prey
Small mammals, such as mice, are an owl's favourite food, and it listens for them moving about on the ground.

Disc face

The disc-like face of a barn owl helps to gather sound waves coming from the prey, and focuses them towards its ears.

Sensitive ears

Owls have one ear slightly higher than the other, which helps them to pin-point the position of prey.

Hunting grip

Like other birds of prey, owls have long claws, called talons, which are good for grabbing their prey.

What helps other animals hunt at night?

Sense of smell

Many furry mammals, such as this European badger, hunt at night. They do so using their excellent sense of smell. They can even sniff out little animals hiding under the ground.

Sensitive eyes

Many night-time hunting mammals, such as cats, have good vision even in dim light. Their eyes have a special layer that reflects and concentrates low levels of light. This makes it seem like their eyes glow in the dark.

Why can't ostriches fly?

The world's biggest bird is just too heavy to fly. Although an ostrich has big, floppy wings, they're not strong enough to flap and lift its body off the ground. Instead, it relies on powerful legs to sprint away from danger.

Balancing wings

Ostrich wings are big but too weak for flight. Instead, they are used to keep balance while running.

Heavy-duty

Ostrich legs have heavy, solid bones unlike the light, hollow bones of birds that fly. They have powerful muscles that are good for running and even kicking hungry predators.

? True or false?

1. Ostriches bury their head in the sand.

2. Ostriches are the fastest animal on two legs.

See pages 134–135 for the answers

Level-headed

An ostrich's head stays level, even when running at top speed. This helps it maintain steady vision to find mates and look out for enemies.

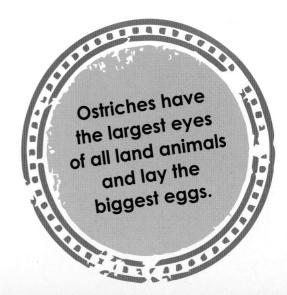

Ostriches have the largest eyes of all land animals and lay the biggest eggs.

Missing bone

Ostriches are missing a part of the breastbone that supports the flight muscles in birds that can fly.

Running feet

Ostriches are the only living birds with just two toes on each foot. This means their feet can clip the ground like a hoof for super-fast sprinting.

What can happen to flightless birds?

Extinction

Dodos lived safely on the island of Mauritius until people arrived. The flightless dodos were easily caught by human hunters until there were none left.

Endangered

Kakapos are flightless parrots that are in danger of becoming extinct. This is because they cannot fly away from predators, such as cats, brought into their habitat by humans.

Why are peacocks such show-offs?

Peacocks show off their colourful feathers to attract and win mates. They fan them out and rustle them to gain attention. The females, called peahens, choose mates according to the size and colour of their feathers.

Spots like eyes

The blue-green spots, or "eyes", grab the female's attention. The peacock turns them towards the peahen so that he has a greater chance of impressing her.

? Quick quiz

1. Which is the closest relative of peacocks?
   a) Bird of paradise
   b) Pheasant
   c) Ostrich

2. Which is the most likely predator of a peacock in the wild?
   a) Tiger
   b) Lion
   c) Crocodile

See pages 134–135 for the answers

Not a tail

The peacock's display feathers grow from the base of the back. When lowered, these feathers sit on top of the bird's tail.

Huge display

There are about 100–150 feathers, and each can be up to 2 m (6½ ft) long. These make up more than half of a peacock's length.

Why do gorillas beat their chests?

Threat display

Display is not all about males impressing females. A male gorilla thumps his chest to look fierce and scare intruders away.

Blending in

Peahens are less colourful than peacocks. They look after the eggs and young, and because of their dull colours, they don't attract predators.

Feather shaft

The white shaft of each feather is a striking contrast to the green and blue, making the bright colours stand out more.

Frequent flyer

Long, pointed wings help to make the tiny Arctic tern a super-efficient flier, so it can cover long distances with ease.

Why do birds migrate?

Many birds fly long distances every year to places with more food in winter and good breeding spots in summer. This is called migration. Arctic terns make the longest migration in the animal world, flying from the Arctic to Antarctica and back again every year.

Migration route

Arctic terns fly south from the Arctic during autumn, reaching Antarctica when it is summer there. They fly back north once it is autumn in Antarctica.

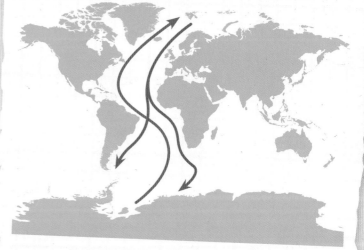

Route from the Arctic to Antarctica

Route from Antarctica to the Arctic

Breeding in the north
Terns raise their young in the Arctic summer, from May to August, when there's lots of food available to feed the chicks.

Resting in the south
From November to February, Arctic terns rest in Antarctica, where it is summer and there is plenty of fish.

Do any other animals migrate?

Monarch butterfly
In the autumn, this American butterfly migrates thousands of kilometres southwards to warmer places, where they hibernate (remain inactive) over the winter.

Caribou
Big herds of American reindeer, called caribou, travel about 5,000 km (3,000 miles) each year. This is the longest overland migration of any animal.

Long journey
On average, an Arctic tern flies at least the same distance as a trip to the Moon and back in its lifetime.

? Quick quiz

1. Why do some birds migrate but others don't?

2. Does migration only involve moving north and south?

3. Do migrations always take place in different seasons?

See pages 134–135 for the answers

Fuelled by fish
The Arctic tern's energy comes from eating fish. As the bird flies southwards towards Antarctica, it dives for fish near coasts. Strong winds help make the northward journey back to the Arctic quicker.

Why don't sleeping birds fall off their perches?

Surprisingly, a treetop perch is a perfectly safe spot for a bird to fall asleep on. When it sits on a branch, its toes automatically curl and lock around it. Even when it is dozing, it never loses its grip.

? Picture quiz

Which bird can go to sleep even while it is flying?

See pages 134–135 for the answer

Sleepy eyes

Birds can sleep with one eye open, and with one half of their brain alert, while the other half rests.

Fluffy feathers

Some birds fluff up their feathers while sleeping to keep their bodies warm.

Foot-locking mechanism

When a bird bends its legs to sit on a branch, tendons – parts of the body that join muscles to bones – automatically pull and lock the toes into a curled position. As long as the leg remains bent, the toes stay locked.

Toes curl around a branch as the leg bends.

How a bird holds onto its perch

Curling toes

Most perching birds have three toes pointing forwards and one backwards. However, parrots, such as these conures from South America, have two front-facing and two back-facing toes.

How do horses sleep?

Standing

By locking their knees, horses can sleep while standing up. Many large mammals do this so they can quickly escape if danger is nearby.

Which bird builds the best nest?

Birds are expert nest-builders, weaving together plant stalks and grass blades to make cups or baskets in which they lay their eggs. Male baya weavers, from Asia, use their strong beaks to make one of the most impressive nests.

Nest to impress

The male baya weaver uses his expert weaving skills to encourage a passing female to choose his nest for her eggs.

Anchored

Baya weavers hang their nests from branches to keep them away from predators that might steal the eggs and young.

? Quick quiz

1. Which bird builds the smallest nest?

2. Do all birds build nests?

3. Which other animals build nests?

See pages 134–135 for the answers

Finishing touches

If a female likes the nest, she will join the male and help build the entrance tunnel.

Cosy corner

The female lines the nest chamber with feathers to make a softer base for her eggs and young.

What else do birds build?

Bower for mating

In Australia, a male bowerbird builds an arrangement of grass and stems called a bower to win a mate. He uses colourful objects as finishing touches and then waits for a female to pass by. If she is impressed, she mates with him.

Clay nests

A swallow scoops mouthfuls of mud and shapes it into a cup, which then hardens into a solid nest. Nests usually hang from a wall or a roof.

Why don't penguins freeze in the snow?

In Antarctica, the world's coldest place, your toes could freeze solid at any moment. Emperor penguins have adapted to survive the icy conditions. They huddle together for warmth and are protected by thick, feathery coats.

Wind barriers

Breeding colonies of penguins sometimes shelter from chilly winds behind ice cliffs.

Group huddle

Emperor penguins and their chicks stand in a huddle to try to stop their body heat from escaping. They face inwards, away from the icy winds, and take turns to stand at the edge.

? *True or false?*

1. The emperor penguin is the world's biggest penguin.

2. The emperor penguin is the only bird to breed in Antarctica.

See pages 134–135 for the answers

Which other animals can fight the frost?

Crocodile icefish

In the freezing Antarctic Ocean, the crocodile icefish stays alive by having special blood. It contains a chemical that stops ice crystals forming in the fish's body.

Wood frog

The North American wood frog freezes most of its body during winters to survive the extreme cold. It thaws to its normal state in warmer weather.

Keeping warm

Dense feathers and an extra-thick layer of fat under the skin help to trap body heat. Feathers also repel water easily, keeping the penguin dry.

During the 2 months a male emperor penguin keeps the egg warm, he doesn't eat anything.

Cold feet

Penguins sometimes lean back onto their stiff tail so that their feet don't touch the frozen ground. This helps to reduce the loss of body heat.

What eats eagles?

The biggest kinds of eagles, such as the bald eagle from North America, are so strong and quick that they are at the top of their food chain. This means that there's nothing else that can kill and eat them.

Eyes
The bald eagle has excellent vision. It can focus on a fish in the water even when flying 300 m (1,000 ft) above the surface.

Which other animals are top predators?

Grizzly bear
The grizzly bear, from North America, is one of the biggest of all land predators. It mostly eats nuts, berries, and fruit, but also preys on rodents and bigger animals, such as deer. The males usually live by themselves, but may gather to feast on fish.

Anaconda
The world's heaviest snake, the anaconda, kills animals the size of small pigs by squeezing them so tight they cannot breathe, before swallowing them whole. It lives in South America, where its diet includes small deer, birds, and turtles.

Food chain

In a food chain, arrows show the direction of energy (in the food) to the top predator. In this case, the tiniest animals in the water, plankton, are eaten by little shrimps called krill. Salmon then eat krill, and bald eagles eat salmon.

Bald eagle

Pink salmon

Krill

Plankton

Tail feathers

Big tail feathers help to control movement as the eagle swoops down to catch prey.

Talons

An eagle's feet have long, curved talons that give them a strong grip for grasping big, slippery fish.

Diet

Big eagles are strong enough to prey on animals the size of a small deer, but a bald eagle's most common prey is fish.

? Quick quiz

1. An eagle kills its prey by…
   a) biting it with its sharp beak
   b) gripping it with its talons
   c) dropping it to the ground

2. What is the weight of a bald eagle's nest?
   a) The weight of a rabbit
   b) The weight of a grown man
   c) The weight of a small car

See pages 134–135 for the answers

Why don't woodpeckers get a headache?

A woodpecker can hammer its beak against a tree trunk 12,000 times a day looking for insects to eat, and not hurt its head. That's because its brain is held snugly inside a skull made of special bone that cushions it from the blows.

How do other animals get food from tree trunks?

Twigs for tools
The woodpecker finch is one of the few birds that uses a tool: it pokes a twig into holes in tree bark to pull out tasty insects.

Finger food
The aye-aye, from Madagascar, taps on a branch, listens for grubs inside, and then uses its finger to scoop them out.

Skull
A woodpecker's skull is made of a thick, spongy bone that absorbs vibrations from the blows. It also has a special bone, called the hyoid, that acts like a seatbelt to hold the skull in place.

Tail prop
Strong, stiff feathers in a woodpecker's tail act as a support. They push back on the trunk while the woodpecker hammers against the upright tree.

Beak

The beak is strong enough for hammering – and its tip can even carry on repairing itself so it doesn't get worn down.

A woodpecker can hit a tree trunk 20 times per second.

..Claws

A woodpecker has clawed toes – two facing forwards and two facing backwards. These help it get a firm grip on the trunk.

? **True or false?**

1. Woodpeckers can even make holes in concrete.

2. Woodpeckers drum on trees to communicate.

3. Woodpeckers make holes in trees for nests.

See pages 134–135 for the answers

Underwater

The world's oceans, lakes, and rivers are home to many different animals. Most have gills to breathe in water but some, such as dolphins, have to come to the surface for air.

See pages 134–135 for the answers

? True or false?

1. Some deep-sea fish produce light.

2. Some rabbits can glow.

Why do jellyfish glow?

Like many other animals of the deep sea, some kinds of jellyfish, such as this mauve stinger, can produce light – perhaps as a way of avoiding being eaten. A soft, juicy jellyfish is a tasty meal for some animals, but a bright flash might dazzle or frighten a hunter.

Glow in the dark

This jellyfish produces light because of a type of chemical reaction that takes place in its body.

Deadly stingers

Jellyfish have stinging cells in their tentacles that they use to paralyse their prey. •••••>

Wriggly tentacles

The tentacles also glow. They are packed with muscle to catch prey and transfer it to the mouth inside the bell. •••••>

Which other animals glow in the dark?

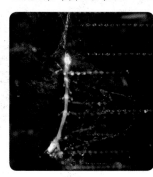

Fungus gnats

Flying insects are attracted to light. The predatory young of the cave-dwelling fungus gnat produce glowing threads of slime to ensnare prey.

Glowworm beetle

These beetles flash light from their rear end. They use flashes to communicate with one another when they are searching for mates.

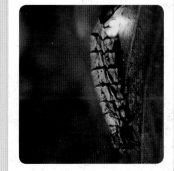

Do fish sleep?

Fish sleep, but because they don't have eyelids, it can be difficult to tell if they are dozing or awake. However, a sleeping parrotfish is easy to spot because it builds a slimy cocoon around itself to sleep in.

Slime blanket

Every night, the parrotfish makes a protective blanket of slime to sleep inside. It produces the slime from its mouth.

The parrotfish takes up to an hour to build its cocoon.

Safe cocoon

The cocoon is a protective shield against bites from bugs, such as fish lice. This may be because it hides the smell of the fish.

Which animals have unusual eyes?

Chameleon

Most reptiles, such as chameleons, have eyelids that are fixed to the pupils. When a chameleon moves an eye, the eyelid moves with it.

Gecko

Like most geckos, a Namib sand gecko does not have eyelids. It keeps its eyes clean by licking them with its long tongue.

? Quick quiz

1. Do all parrotfish build a night-time cocoon?

2. Do all fish sleep at night?

See pages 134–135 for the answers

Predator alarm

The slimy blanket may also act as an early warning system against predators. The fish gets time to swim away when predators, such as moray eels, disturb the cocoon.

How do pufferfish puff up?

For a fish that is a mouth-sized snack for a bigger fish, a good way to defend yourself is to get bigger. The pufferfish does just that, by swallowing water. Some are also poisonous.

Small and slow

Pufferfish are slow and clumsy swimmers, and when deflated, like this one, can be quite small. This makes them an easy target for predators.

? Quick quiz

1. Do pufferfish have teeth?

2. How do baby pufferfish defend themselves?

3. How does a pufferfish deflate?

See pages 134–135 for the answers

Split-proof

A pufferfish's skin is tough and stretchy, so it doesn't split when the fish puffs up. Its stomach has folded walls, which allows it to expand.

More than a mouthful

An inflated pufferfish not only looks scary, but is also too big to fit in the mouth of many predators. This is important because it swims twice as slowly when puffed up.

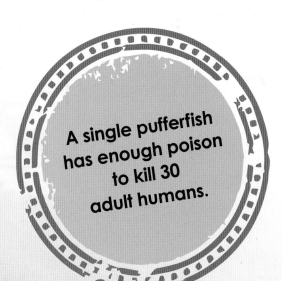

A single pufferfish has enough poison to kill 30 adult humans.

Which other animals huff and puff?

Toad

If a toad feels threatened, it gulps extra air into its lungs and stretches its legs to appear bigger and scarier.

Frigate bird

Male frigate birds puff up their bright red throat pouch, just like a balloon, to impress females.

Can flying fish really fly?

Flying fish soar above water on their wide fins, which makes them look like they are flying. They pick up speed underwater and then jump above the surface to escape predators. However, since they can't flap their fins, they glide rather than actually fly.

Folded down

The flying fish keeps its side fins in a folded position until it breaks the surface. The fins then expand into gliders.

Leaping to safety

A flying fish has so much power in its muscles that it can leap about 6 m (20 ft) into the air.

Picture quiz

Which squid can glide above the surface of the water?

See pages 134–135 for the answer

Speedy tail

The forked tailfin quivers up to 70 times a second to launch the flying fish out of the water.

Stiff body

The torpedo-shaped body is held straight, making it easier for the fish to glide through the air. It can stay in the air for up to 45 seconds.

Fins for wings

The fish opens its front side fins to use like wings. Some flying fish have extra-big rear fins, too.

A flying fish can glide up to 70 kph (43 mph) through the air.

Which other animals seem to fly?

Flying squirrel

This animal has furry skin that stretches from its wrists to its ankles. This works like a parachute as the squirrel glides from one tree to another.

Flying frog

While most frogs are experts at the long jump, Wallace's flying frog can glide from trees using its broad webbed feet.

A hammerhead has up to 3,000 sensory pores on its head.

How do sharks find prey?

Some sharks are good at sensing blood in the water, but all of them have an even smarter method for tracking prey. Using special sensors, they can detect the tiny electrical signals inside an animal's working muscles and nerves.

? True or false?

1. All sharks are man-eaters.

2. Sharks keep producing new teeth during their lifetime.

See pages 134–135 for the answers

Wide-eyed wonder

The hammerhead's eyes are placed far apart, on the tips of the "hammer". This gives the shark a 360° view around it.

Can any animal use electricity to shock?

Torpedo ray

The torpedo ray's flat body is packed with organs that can generate an electric shock to keep away predators.

Electric eel

Although all animals produce electricity in their muscles and nerves, the electric eel can produce bigger electric shocks to stun prey.

Buried prey

Hammerhead sharks often snack on stingrays, which hide by burying themselves in the sand. A shark finds them by using its "hammer" like a metal detector to scan the bottom.

Hammerhead

The hammerhead shark's strange-looking head is packed with tiny sensors along its front edge. These detect electrical activity from prey.

Is coral alive?

Coral might look like colourful rocks, but in fact it's a colony (group) of tiny living animals called polyps. During the day, the coral looks lifeless. At night, however, thousands of polyps stretch out their tentacles to catch and feed on tiny animals drifting in the water.

Coral reef

A coral reef's surface is peppered with thousands of polyps. They are rooted to a fixed spot, but can still wave their tentacles.

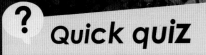

? Quick quiz

1. How does coral sting?

2. What is a coral reef?

See pages 134–135 for the answers

Single polyp

An open polyp looks like an anemone. A ring of stinging tentacles catch and paralyse tiny prey, then moves it to the mouth at the centre.

Rocky skeleton

Much of the coral is made of hard, rocky skeleton, which protects the soft parts of the animals inside.

The world's first coral reefs formed about 500 million years ago.

Which other animals look lifeless?

Stonefish

This fish looks like a lump of rock, but the spines on its back can give you a terrible sting.

Sea sponges

Sponges also live in a colony, but don't have tentacles. If they are broken apart, the bits can even group back together.

Why do dolphins have blowholes?

Just like us, a dolphin must breathe air with its lungs, even though it spends its life swimming in water. It uses a blowhole to inhale air at the surface, and then holds its breath when it goes underwater.

? Quick quiz

1. Which other marine mammal uses a blowhole?
   a) Whale
   b) Seal
   c) Sea otter

2. How high can dolphins leap into the air?
   a) 3 m (10 ft)
   b) 4.5 m (15 ft)
   c) 6 m (20 ft)

See pages 134–135 for the answers

Blowing bubbles

Dolphins blow streams of bubbles from their blowhole. They do this while hunting to confuse fish by clouding the water and making it hard to see.

Blowhole

The blowhole works like a nostril for breathing in air. A special valve closes the blowhole when the dolphin is underwater.

Dolphins can usually hold their breath for about 3 to 7 minutes.

Deep breath

The dolphin's body has more blood than a similar-sized human. This means it can carry higher levels of oxygen, helping it stay longer underwater on each breath.

Feeding

Unlike humans, dolphins never breathe through their mouth. They have separate paths for food and air so that their lungs don't flood with water while they are eating.

How do other air-breathing animals breathe in water?

Air bubbles

The water spider is the only spider that hunts underwater. It keeps breathing by creating a silk-lined bubble of air, a bit like how a deep-sea diver carries a tank of oxygen.

Upturned noses

Hippopotamuses have their nostrils high on their head. This means they can keep breathing even if most of their body is underwater.

What animals live in the deep sea?

More than 1,000 m (3,000 ft) below the surface, the ocean is bitterly cold and pitch black. Many strange deep-sea creatures are perfectly suited to make this harsh place their home.

? Quick quiz

1. Which animal lives deepest in the ocean?

2. How do scientists know what lives in the deep sea?

See pages 134–135 for the answers

Dumbo octopus

Unlike other octopuses, the dumbo octopus has ear-like flaps that help it swim. It lives about 3,000 m (10,000 ft) below the ocean's surface.

Fangtooth

This fish has teeth so big that it cannot completely close its jaws. It grabs prey with the fangs and swallows the fish whole.

Which animals can survive extremely hot conditions?

Giant kangaroo rat

Some animals that live in hot, dry grasslands – such as the giant kangaroo rat from California, USA – can survive in this tough environment without ever having a drop of water to drink. It gets all the water it needs from its food.

Saharan ant

Most animals would die in places where the ground is hot enough to cook an egg on. However, this desert ant can scamper between its burrows over sand that's more than 50°C (122°F) in the burning sun.

Anglerfish

The female anglerfish uses a glowing lantern on her head to attract other fish. They swim towards to the light, and are quickly gulped up.

Pelican eel

Food is hard to find in the deep sea. To survive, this fish uses its enormous jaws to scoop up shoals of prey, such as shrimp, in one go.

Why don't clownfish get stung by sea anemones?

A stinging sea anemone might seem a strange place to set up home, but clownfish have an extra-slimy coating for protection. Living in the anemone keeps the clownfish safe from predators, and in return the fish keep the anemone clean and drive away its enemies.

Slimy skin

All fish are covered in slime, but it is three times as thick on a clownfish. This protects it from the venomous sting of the anemone.

Enemies

Clownfish are protective of their anemone home. They will chase away other kinds of fish, such as the butterfly fish, which eat anemones.

? Quick quiz

1. Why do sea anemones sting?

2. Are other fish protected by slime?

3. Are anemones animals?

See pages 134–135 for the answers

Which other animals can resist venom?

Mongoose
A cobra's bite is usually enough to kill a small animal. However, the mongoose – a type of mammal – is unaffected by the cobra's venom so ends up with snake for dinner.

Honey badger
You must get past angry bees to steal honey from a bee's nest. But a honey badger has such thick skin that it isn't bothered by the bees' stings.

Hide-and-seek
Eels and other predators can't attack clownfish when they hide in the anemone's tentacles.

Clean up
While the anemone feeds on the poo of clownfish, the clownfish clean up dead tentacles and the leftovers from the anemone's meals.

Why do crabs walk sideways?

We walk forwards because our knees bend at the front. But most crabs have wide shells that make their leg joints point towards the side instead. This means they find it easier to walk sideways.

Bendy joints

Crabs have several joints in each leg. Each can bend, like our knees, making the legs extra flexible.

Which other animals have funny walks?

Batfish

Batfish have flat bodies shaped like tennis rackets. They use their flap-like fins for walking slowly on the seabed.

Grebes

A grebe's feet are positioned far back on its body. This makes them good for paddling in the water, but on land they make this bird walk awkwardly.

Some crabs have "teeth" inside their stomachs to help break down food.

Watchful eyes

This ghost crab has especially big eyes for spotting danger, so it can get ready to run.

Legs on the side

A crab has four pairs of legs attached to the side of its body, and two claws in front, facing forwards.

Which snake moves sideways by making S-shaped curves?

See pages 134–135 for the answer

Sand lines

As a crab scurries sideways over sand, its feet make lines that run alongside one another.

Are piranhas bloodthirsty?

Piranhas have razor-sharp teeth for eating meat. Many stories describe them as very aggressive fish that attack in large groups and will tear any creature to pieces, including humans. However, piranhas actually prefer to prey on other fish and they probably gather in groups for safety, not to hunt and kill.

? True or false?

1. Piranhas live in South America.

2. All types of piranhas only eat meat.

3. Piranhas are most active at night.

See pages 134–135 for the answers

Power bite

As well as having sharp teeth, piranhas have extra-strong jaws – giving them a dangerous bite.

Which animals are actually bloodthirsty?

Vampire bat

This bat uses its sharp teeth to make a cut in its victim's skin. Then, it laps up the blood that flows from the wound. It has a heat sensor on its nose that helps it locate the spot from where the victim's warm blood flows.

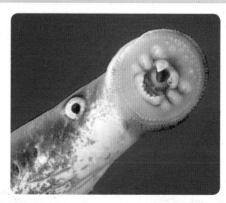

Lamprey

Instead of biting jaws, this fish has a circular mouth ringed with teeth. The mouth clamps onto another fish's body and sucks out the blood.

Racing ahead

Like most fish, a piranha gets much of its swimming power from beating its tail from side to side.

A piranha can bite right through the finger of a careless fisherman.

Safety in numbers

Piranhas stay in large groups called "schools". This protects them from enemies as predators find it difficult to single out a victim from a big group.

Breathing

Whales, like these sperm whales, must come up to the surface for air, where they may be harmed by colliding with ships.

Wrong signals

Signals from submarines can interfere with the communication between whales, stopping them from diving or feeding.

Diving to eat

Sperm whales can dive more than 2 km (1.2 miles) down – deeper than almost any other kind of mammal. Here, they hunt for their favourite prey, deep-water squid.

At their peak, in around 1950, whaling ships killed 25,000 sperm whales per year.

How many whales are there in the ocean?

The world's oceans are home to many different types of whales, but hunting by humans means there are fewer whales alive today than a century ago. Many species are endangered, which means they could soon die out completely. There are hundreds of thousands of sperm whales, but perhaps only 10,000 blue whales left in the ocean.

Endangered species

These are some of the endangered whales.

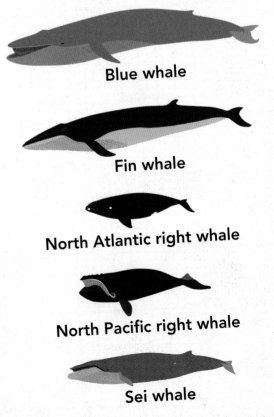

Blue whale

Fin whale

North Atlantic right whale

North Pacific right whale

Sei whale

Why do animals become endangered?

Hunting
If animals are hunted by humans faster than they can breed, their numbers decline. Black rhinos have nearly been wiped out because they are killed for their horns.

Loss of home
The Philippine eagle lives in rainforests, but deforestation (cutting down forests) has reduced the number of places where it can live and find food.

Creepy-crawlies

Animals without a backbone, such as insects, spiders, and snails, are called invertebrates. There are more kinds of creepy-crawly in the world than any other type of animal.

Why don't pond-skaters sink?

While others insects may drown, pond-skaters dart easily across the water. Special foot pads with waxy hairs stop them sinking. The pond-skater's feet dent the water's surface, but the waterproof hairs keep them dry.

The skater's sensitive feet pick up the vibrations of drowning insects for it to eat.

Back legs

As the pond-skater skims over the water, it uses its back legs like rudders to make high-speed turns when chasing prey.

Which other animals can move across the water's surface?

Sprinting above
This basilisk lizard, from Central and South America, is probably the heaviest animal that can walk on water. Its feet cup bubbles of air to keep it afloat, but it needs to run fast to prevent itself from sinking.

Hanging below
The surface "skin" of water can support tiny animals underneath the water, as well as above it. The predatory backswimmer hugs the skin while it reloads a store of air it keeps under its wings. It uses this air when diving for prey.

Front legs
The spiny front legs are used for grabbing insect prey. Pond-skaters have piercing, beak-like mouthparts that contain poisonous spit, which leaves prey unable to move.

Middle legs
The pond skater's middle legs are used like oars. They push the insect across the pond's surface.

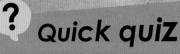

? Quick quiz

1. Why do flies, unlike pond-skaters, drown in water?

2. Why are all water-walking animals small?

3. Can other animals walk on water?

See pages 134–135 for the answers

Why do honeybees dance?

It takes a lot of nectar to feed an entire honeybee hive, so when a bee finds some nectar-rich flowers, she shares her knowledge. Back at the hive, she performs a "waggle dance", which tells the other bees the location of the flowers.

Wings
The buzzing sound of a bee is made by the flapping of its wings.

Together, a hive's bees can visit 40 flowers each minute.

The waggle dance

The returning bee performs a figure-of-eight dance move, which tells other bees the direction they must fly in to find the nectar. The faster the dance, the closer the nectar is.

This is the direction the bees must fly in relation to the sun.

Others bees gather around to watch the dance.

? True or false?

1. All bees are female.

2. Honeybees hibernate in the winter.

3. Honeybees need both nectar and pollen for food.

See pages 134–135 for the answers

Drinking nectar

The bee drinks nectar from a flower's nectar-producing parts by using a special hairy tongue.

Pollen sac

Flowers produce tiny grains of pollen to make seeds. Bees like to eat pollen. They collect it in a sac and fix it to a groove on their back legs to take home.

Sting

Bees use their jagged, venomous sting to defend the hive.

Which other animals dance?

Peacock spider

The male peacock spider from Australia waves his body and legs in a very colourful dance to impress a female.

Bird of paradise

Many birds of paradise have amazingly colourful feathers. Males, like this Western parotia, perform dances to attract females.

Why do dung beetles collect poo?

There's got to be a good reason to roll a dung ball that's ten times heavier than your body, but it's all in a day's work for a dung beetle dad. He collects other animal's poo to eat and to feed his young. Sometimes the mum even rides on top of the dung ball while he pushes it along.

Which other animals clean up?

Gravedigger
Sexton beetles bury dead animals, such as mice, and lay their eggs on the dead bodies so food is available when they hatch.

Leftovers
Scavenging vultures pick over the skin and bones left over from the kills of lions and other predators.

Wings
The dung beetle's front wings are hard and shell-like. They cover up a second pair that are used for flying around to find dung.

Look out behind
Beetles roll the dung with their middle and back legs, while the first pair grips the ground.

Dung dinner

Dung beetle parents work together to bury the ball of dung. The mum then lays an egg inside it. The baby that hatches out feasts on the dung so it can grow into an adult beetle.

Precious poo

The beetle dad fights off other dung beetles that try to steal his ball.

? Quick quiz

1. What would happen if there were no dung beetles?

2. How do dung beetles make dung into a ball?

3. Do dung beetle parents look after their children?

See pages 134–135 for the answers

Why are ants so busy?

No one can rest in an ant colony. Thousands of workers come and go to look after their nest. They must collect food, look after the young, and defend the colony. Deep inside their home the queen is busy too, laying eggs that will become new workers.

A leaf-cutter ant can carry 50 times its body weight.

Worker ants

Workers carry the fragments of leaf above their bodies. Spines on their back help support the load.

Piece of leaf

After neatly cutting out a piece of leaf with their jaws, a strong leaf-cutter worker takes it back to the nest.

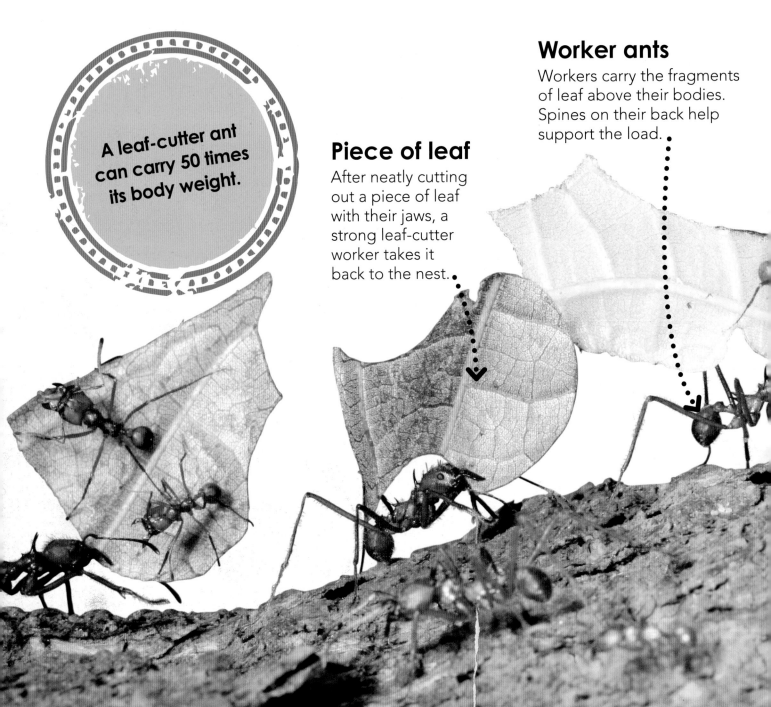

In the colony

Ant queens are much larger than workers. They lay all the colonies' eggs, but the workers look after them.

Soldiers are workers that have big heads with strong jaws. Their job is to defend the colony.

All workers are female. Workers collect leaves for the nest and the tiniest ones grow fungus on the leaves to feed the colony.

Queen

Soldier

Worker

? Quick quiz

1. Do worker ants lay eggs?

2. When do ants fly?

3. Do all ants collect leaves?

See pages 134–135 for the answers

Cleaning up
Some workers ride along, and make sure the leaf is clean and pest-free.

Fungus food
Workers bring leaf fragments back to the nest's "larder". Smaller workers grow fungi on the leaves as food.

What other animals are ruled by a queen?

Termites
These white-bodied, ant-like insects build huge towers out of clay to house their colony. A termite queen can grow up to 15 cm (6 in) long.

Naked mole rats
These African mammals live underground in societies ruled by a queen. She mates with one or two males and, just like ants, her non-breeding daughter "workers" look after the burrow.

Why do lice live in our hair?

Your head makes a comfortable home for certain insects, and can even provide them with food. A head louse grips your hair with its legs and uses its sharp mouthparts to puncture the skin when it's hungry, to drink your blood. Lice cannot fly, so stay on your body, gluing their egg cases to your hair.

Magnified

Head lice are about 2–3 mm (0.08–0.1 in) long. This image has been magnified about 100 times.

A head louse bites 4 or 5 times per day.

Which other animals can feed on our bodies?

Tapeworm

A tapeworm can live inside your intestine (gut), where it absorbs some of your digested food. It gets there if you eat meat that is infected with tapeworm egg capsules. Some tapeworms can be as long as 10 m (33 ft).

Leech

Leeches are worms that feed by biting skin and drinking blood. Once full, the leech drops off until hunger drives it to find a new victim. They live in water and on land.

Mouthparts

The louse sticks out needles from its head, which it uses to puncture the skin to suck up blood.

Claws

Clawed legs help keep a tight grip on a hair. The louse moves slowly and has no wings, so cannot fly.

Body

When the louse feeds, its abdomen (body) swells up as the stomach inside becomes filled with blood.

? True or false?

1. Nits are louse eggs.

2. Lice prefer dirty hair to clear hair.

3. Lice can move between human heads.

See pages 134–135 for the answers

How does a spider make a web?

Spiders spin their webs using a special thread called silk. It is finer than human hair but stronger than steel and is perfect for trapping unsuspecting insects. Spiders create almost-invisible nets between leaves, then scatter them with sticky blobs so anything that flies into the web can't escape.

Orb-weaver

The European garden spider is an orb-weaving spider, which means it builds circular webs. It makes a new one each day.

Spinnerets

Silk starts off as a runny goo in a spider's rear end. It squirts out through special nozzles called spinnerets – a process a bit like squeezing glue out of a tube. Then it hardens into silk threads.

How to build a web

1. The spider releases a thread of silk, which is carried on a breeze until it fastens onto an object. The spider then releases a second thread to create a Y-shape.

2. The spider adds more silk threads running from the centre outwards. These are like the spokes of a wheel, and make sure the web has a strong frame.

3. The spider spins a spiral of threads from the middle outwards to strengthen the web. Then it works back towards the centre adding a sticky spiral for trapping prey.

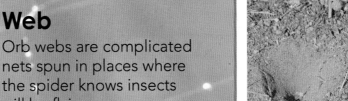

<------....... Web
Orb webs are complicated nets spun in places where the spider knows insects will be flying.

? Quick quiz

1. Do spiders use silk for anything else?

2. What is the biggest web in the world?

3. What are "cobwebs"?

See pages 134–135 for the answers

Which other animals use traps?

Antlion
An antlion larva (juvenile) catches its prey by digging a sandpit. It waits buried at the bottom and uses its big jaws to grab ants that fall in.

Black heron
Black herons create a shadow by making "umbrellas" with their wings. This lures in nervous fish that think they are safe by hiding in the shade.

What's inside a snail's shell?

A snail carries its home on its back. The shell protects its soft body and vital organs, such as the heart. Deep within the shell, the snail's body is attached to a spiral chamber by a muscle. This pulls the snail inside at the first sign of danger.

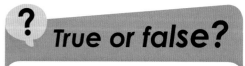

? True or false?

1. A slug is simply a snail without a shell.

2. Garden snails are vegetarian.

3. Some snails breathe using gills.

See pages 134–135 for the answers

Garden snails are neither male nor female – they have both kinds of sex organs.

Shell
The shell is made from hard chalky and horn-like substances.

Eyes

A typical garden snail has eyes on the ends of tentacles to see what's happening outside the shell.

Muscular foot

The snail has a single foot for creeping forwards. It is packed with rippling muscles to pull the snail and its shell along.

Inside the shell

A snail's vital organs, such as its lung and heart, stay hidden inside the shell. Only its head and muscular foot come out, so it can get around and sense the surroundings.

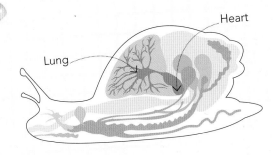

Heart

Lung

Do other animals carry their homes?

Turtles

A shell is like a suit of armour for turtles and tortoises. Some can even pull their head and feet inside.

Hermit crabs

Most crabs grow a hard shell, but not hermit crabs. Instead, they use empty snail shells to protect their soft bodies.

How do mosquitoes find their prey?

It's no wonder we struggle to keep mosquitoes away. They find us by smelling the carbon dioxide in the air we breathe out. When they get closer, they home in on our warm, sweaty skin. You only need to watch out for females, though, as the males don't drink blood.

A mosquito can spend 2 to 3 minutes feeding on blood.

Antennae

The female mosquito's antennae (feelers) detect the smell of a victim. Males have bushier antennae for finding females. They feed on nectar, not blood.

Stabbing mouthparts

The female's mouthparts are long and sharp for piercing the skin's surface.

Wings

The mosquito uses a single pair of wings to fly around and find her victim. The wings lie flat along the body when not in use.

1. Do all mosquitoes feed on blood?

2. Can blood-sucking mosquitoes be dangerous?

3. Why do mosquito bites itch?

See pages 134–135 for the answers

Blood

As the mosquito feeds, the blood passes into its stomach, making its body swell up and turn red.

What other insects have super senses?

Emperor moths

Male emperor moths are champions at smelling. Males can even find a female when she is 10 km (6 miles) away. It's just as well – the moths don't live long and have just one month to find a mate.

Black fire beetles

Most animals run from forest fires, but not the black fire beetle. It has sensors that attract it to heat and flames. The beetle then lays its eggs in the dead charred wood.

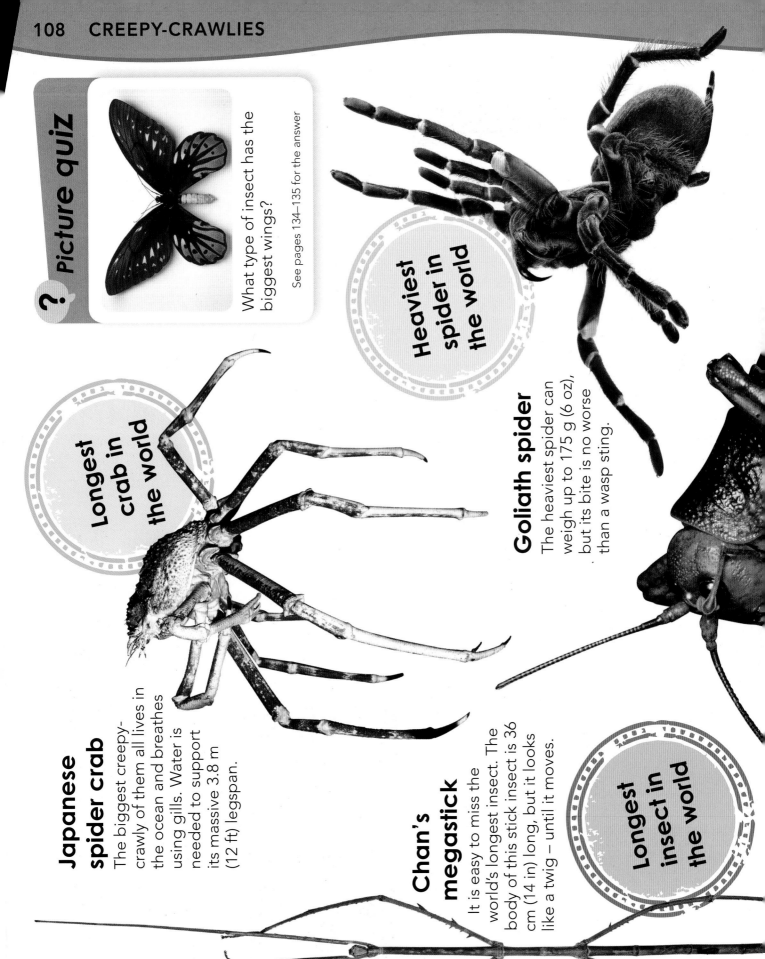

Picture quiz

What type of insect has the biggest wings?

See pages 134–135 for the answer

Heaviest spider in the world

Goliath spider

The heaviest spider can weigh up to 175 g (6 oz), but its bite is no worse than a wasp sting.

Longest crab in the world

Japanese spider crab

The biggest creepy-crawly of them all lives in the ocean and breathes using gills. Water is needed to support its massive 3.8 m (12 ft) legspan.

Chan's megastick

It is easy to miss the world's longest insect. The body of this stick insect is 36 cm (14 in) long, but it looks like a twig – until it moves.

Longest insect in the world

Giant weta

The world's heaviest insect is a type of cricket that lives in New Zealand. A female weta packed with eggs can be three times heavier than a mouse.

Heaviest insect in the world

What is the world's biggest creepy-crawly?

The world is filled with tiny creepy-crawlies, but some can grow to huge sizes. The word "biggest" can refer to different things. We can use it to mean an animal's length, width, or weight. The giants on this page are about as big as creepy-crawlies can get.

How do grasshoppers sing?

The loud chirps of grasshoppers can fill the air on a summer's day. The males of this insect sing to attract females, but they don't use their mouths. Most have little combs on their legs and chirp by rubbing them against their wings. Crickets sing in a similar way, but rub their wings together.

Feelers

Antennae (feelers) detect scents and may even help males know if a female is nearby.

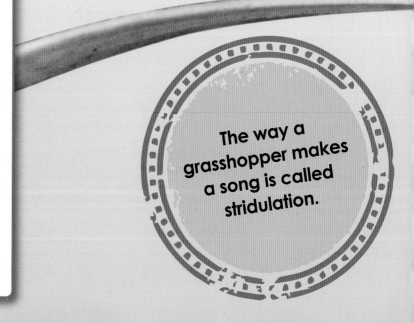

Which other animals sing?

Whistling whales

Beluga whales sing so sweetly that they have been called the "canaries of the sea". They whistle by moving air under their blowholes. They do this to communicate with one another.

Mouse maestro

Like grasshoppers, male mice sing songs to attract females. If a male mouse thinks that a female is nearby, he will sing louder. But you are unlikely to hear him. His song is too high-pitched for human ears to hear.

The way a grasshopper makes a song is called stridulation.

❓ Quick quiz

1. Do any other animals make sounds in the same way as a grasshopper?

2. Do grasshoppers all sound the same?

3. What are the noisiest insects?

See pages 134–135 for the answers

File

A comb-like ridge on each hind leg, called a file, is scraped against part of the wing to make the chirping sound.

Scraper

Grasshoppers have two pairs of wings. The front pair have scrapers, which make sounds when the files are rubbed against them.

Listening for chirps

Grasshoppers listen to each other's songs using two "ears" on their sides. These are actually thin pieces of skin that vibrate when sound hits them.

Reptiles and amphibians

Reptiles and amphibians are cold-blooded. Reptiles have dry and scaly skin, while amphibians are moist and slimy.

How do geckos walk upside down?

Geckos are small lizards that have an amazing ability: they can walk up walls and upside down along ceilings. Special pads on their feet help them cling to smooth surfaces, such as leaves or glass.

Sticky toes

Hairlike bristles on the underside of a gecko's toes are so tiny that you would need a microscope to see them.

Lightweight body

Most geckos are no bigger than a mouse. Millions of sticky bristles on their toes provide enough grip to hold their weight without falling.

Tiny claws

A wall-climbing gecko only has tiny claws because these are not needed to grip smooth, flat surfaces.

Specialized feet

The toes of a gecko's feet end in wide pads for clinging onto surfaces.

See pages 134–135 for the answers

? Quick quiz

1. Why do geckos need to climb?

2. Can all geckos climb walls and ceilings?

3. How did geckos get their name?

Which other animals are good climbers?

Alpine ibex

This goat lives on the Alps mountains in Europe. Its hooves can spread outwards, giving it a good grip on near-vertical rock surfaces.

Housefly

Houseflies and other insects have bristly pads on their feet to help them stick to walls, just like geckos do.

How do chameleons change colour?

Chameleons can change their colour as easily as you can nod your head. They do it by moving around tiny crystals that lie under their skin. Different colours indicate what mood they are in.

Red for display

The male chameleon can flash red to show that he is in an excited mood. This either warns off other males or can attract females.

It's done with mirrors

Some of the chameleon's colour comes from crystals under the skin that act like tiny mirrors to reflect light. When the chameleon is excited, the crystals spread further apart, changing the skin from bluish green to yellowish red.

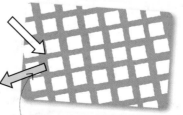

Tightly packed crystals reflect more blue light.

Widely separated crystals reflect more red light.

Green to hide

The chameleon's skin is green when it is relaxed. This helps it to hide among leaves.

Rotating eyes

Chameleons have good colour vision to spot the moods of other chameleons. Each eye can rotate independently of the other.

Which other animals can change colour?

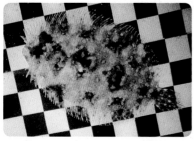

Flatfish

Some flatfish, such as this flounder, are so good at changing colour that they can match the pattern of the background they have settled on.

Golden tortoise beetle

This beetle can change colour from golden to red with spots to scare off birds and other predators who think it could make a tasty snack.

Why do snakes stick their tongue out?

They might look rude, but snakes have a good reason to flick their tongue out. As well as tasting things, a snake's tongue is used to pick up smells in the air – such as the scent of fresh prey.

Looking around
Snakes have fairly good vision, but it is usually not good enough to track prey.

? Quick quiz

1. Are all snakes hunters?

2. Do snakes use other methods to find prey?

See pages 134–135 for the answers

What else do animals use their tongue for?

Cooling

When a dog pants and sticks out its tongue, the moisture on the surface of the tongue evaporates. This helps to cool the body down.

Grooming

A wet tongue is as good as a wash cloth for cleaning. A tiger's tongue even has bristles, so the tiger can give itself a good scrub, too.

Hunting

A chameleon's tongue can flick out so far and so fast that it's perfect for grabbing insects. The tip of the tongue has a sucker, so the chameleon's dinner can't wriggle free.

Jacobson's organ

The tongue transfers scent to a tasting pad, called the Jacobson's organ, in the roof of the snake's mouth.

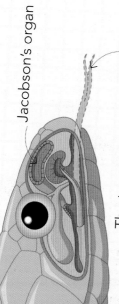

Jacobson's organ

The tongue's tip collects scent particles in the air.

Forked tongue

The forked tip picks up scents coming from both sides, so the snake can tell which direction the scent is coming from.

A snake's lower jaw bones can stretch apart to swallow large prey.

What is an axolotl?

An axolotl, a kind of salamander, is a lizard-like amphibian that never grows up. Other salamanders start as tadpoles with gills, before developing lungs so that they can breathe on land. The axolotl, however, keeps its gills and spends its entire life in water.

Thin-skinned

An axolotl's skin is so soft and thin that it can let oxygen straight through into the bloodstream.

? Quick quiz

1. Do axolotls have skeletons?

2. Are axolotls endangered?

See pages 134–135 for the answers

Feathery gills

An axolotl mainly uses its feathery gills to breathe in water. It also gets rid of some of its body waste through its gills.

In the wild, axolotls are found only in two lakes on the outskirts of Mexico City, Mexico.

Regrowth

Animals can usually repair wounds after injury, but axolotls can regrow entire lost limbs.

Which other animals never grow up?

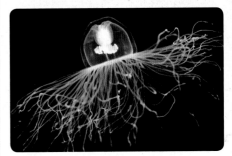

Immortal jellyfish

This tiny jellyfish can settle on the seabed and turn back into its anemone-like baby form to start its development all over again. So perhaps it can live forever!

Wingless aphids

Aphids are insects that suck sap. When lots of food is available, they produce babies that never grow wings – because they don't need to fly away to find food.

Are dragons real?

The fire-breathing dragons that you find in storybooks don't exist in the real world, but a different kind of dragon does. Named after the island in Indonesia where it lives, the Komodo dragon is the world's biggest lizard.

? Picture quiz

Which tiny beetle sprays hot, fiery liquid from its bottom to warn off attackers?

See pages 134–135 for the answer

A Komodo dragon can grow to the size of a crocodile.

Forked tongue

The Komodo dragon is the largest predator on its island. It flicks its forked tongue to pick up the scent of prey several kilometres away.

Heavyweight

The biggest Komodo dragons are heavier than a grown man, and powerful enough to bring down animals the size of a deer.

Which other animals look like dragons?

Frilled lizard

When this Australian lizard senses danger, it raises a big neck frill, which encircles its head to make it look bigger.

Flying dragon

By stretching its expandable ribs, this lizard can open up flaps along its body. It uses them to glide between trees.

Tough skin

Like all reptiles, and the dragons in stories, a Komodo dragon's skin is covered in hard scales. These act like armour in battles with other animals over food.

Deadly claws

Like a storybook dragon, a Komodo dragon has long, sharp claws for ripping open the hides of big prey.

Why are poison dart frogs so colourful?

Poison dart frogs are so brightly coloured that they look like jewels on the floor of their rainforest habitat. But their colours do more than make them look beautiful – they warn hungry predators to stay away. These frogs can be deadly poisonous.

? *True or false?*

1. All poison dart frogs are deadly.

2. Captive poison dart frogs can lose their poisons over time.

See pages 134–135 for the answers

Different colours

This strawberry poison dart frog gets its name from its red skin, but some individuals are yellow or blue.

Deadly slime

The poison dart frog's poisons are in the slime that covers the surface of its body.

Crawling diet

Poison dart frogs get their poisons by eating certain kinds of tiny creepy-crawlies, such as mites (like the one shown here) or ants.

Why else do animals use colour?

Warning

A morpho butterfly's wings are brilliant blue on the upper surface. A quick flash of colour when it opens its wings can startle and scare off insect-eating birds.

Hunting

The colour of an orchid mantis matches the flower it sits on. This helps it hide so it can grab unsuspecting insects coming for nectar.

How long does a tortoise live?

Tortoises really do live life in the slow lane. Their large shell makes them move slowly and their cold-blooded body works at a gentler pace than ours – so it takes longer to wear out. It means that giant tortoises may live for more than a century.

Old legs

Very old tortoises can get arthritis (painful joints). This can slow down their walking. •••••

Which other animals live a long time?

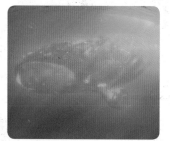

Long-lived giant

All whales live for a long time, but the bowhead whale lives the longest – and far longer than any other kind of mammal. Some individuals could still be breeding after a century and may live for 200 years.

A long reign

Insects don't usually live very long, but a termite queen may live up to 50 years. She spends her life deep inside a termite mound, producing eggs that develop into the workers of the termite's colony.

Growth rings

The plates of a tortoise shell get wider as the animal grows, sometimes making a ring every year – a bit like a tree trunk.

? Picture quiz

Which birds can spend a 40-year lifetime together?

See pages 134–135 for the answer

Tough scales

Like other reptiles, tortoises have scaly skin. The scales have a tough, horny coating, which flakes off as it is replaced from below.

A giant tortoise who died in a zoo in 2006 may have hatched from its egg in 1750.

Do reptiles have cold blood?

Reptiles are often described as "cold-blooded", but their body temperature changes with their surroundings. On a cool day, a reptile has cold blood, but it warms up in the sun. If lizards are too cold, their muscles are slow and they cannot run about.

There are over 10,000 species of reptile, and most of these are found in the hot tropics.

Heating up and cooling down

Heating up

Reptiles, such as this turtle, love to bask in the sun. They use the sun's heat to warm up, helping to make them more active.

Cooling down

Some reptiles can overheat if they stay in the sun too long. Crocodiles open their mouths to cool down. They lose heat from the inside of their mouths, like a panting dog.

? *True or false?*

1. Are there any reptiles found in cold parts of the world?

2. How do ocean reptiles stay warm?

3. Which other animals are "cold-blooded"?

See pages 134–135 for the answers

Eyes for daylight

Being active in the heat of the day means lizards can see to find food and mates. Some have better vision than most mammals.

Scaly skin

Lizards and other reptiles are covered in hard scales that stop their skin from drying out under the hot sun.

Thermal imaging

This picture of a lizard is called a thermal image. The special camera shows the different temperatures in different colours. The sun has warmed some parts of the lizard's body (which look orange), but other parts are still cool (purple).

Sun bed

On cold mornings, reptiles often find a sunny spot, such as on top of a boulder, to warm up quickly. This is called basking.

Some poisonous frogs produce slime that is deadly to humans.

Why are frogs slimy?

If you've ever tried to grab a frog, you'll know how slippery it can be. A frog's skin oozes with slime. It stops the skin from drying out, but also helps to protect it from infection. Some frogs have bitter poisons in their slime to scare away predators, while others use their slime to makes nests for their eggs.

Gripping feet

The slime on the frog's toes helps it to stick to leaves and branches. The frog lays its eggs on high branches to protect them from any egg-eating animals below.

? Quick quiz

1. Why aren't snakes and lizards slimy?

2. Do humans produce slime?

3. Does a frog's slime wash off when it rains?

See pages 134–135 for the answers

Back legs

The frog uses its back legs to smear the slime from its body and mix it with air to make tiny bubbles of foam.

Tadpoles

The eggs hatch into swimming tadpoles. They drop in the pool of water below the nest, where they develop into frogs.

Slimy foam

Forest green tree frogs whip slime into a froth for their eggs. The outer surface hardens to protect the moist eggs inside.

Other slimy creatures

Snail

The slime produced by a snail makes a slippery carpet to help keep its muscular foot sliding forwards. It leaves a tell-tale trail behind it.

Hagfish

The world's slimiest animal uses slime to clog the gills of fish that want to eat it. A single hagfish can produce a bucketful of slime in just minutes.

Do crocodiles really cry?

Tearful eyes don't always mean that an animal is feeling sad. Crocodiles don't cry when they're upset, but like humans they shed tears to stop their eyes drying out. These tears help to keep their eyes clean, too.

Scaly skin
Crocodiles are covered in tough, waterproof scales.

Do any animals feel human emotions?

Laughing hyenas
Hyenas make giggling sounds when they are scared or excited, not because they are happy. They even giggle when they are being bullied by other members of their group.

Mourning elephants
Some scientists think that elephants feel sadness like humans do. When a member of the herd dies, elephants may stay with their dead companion for a short time, and even cry "real" tears.

Look out
A crocodile's eyes are high on its head so it can still see when the rest of its body is in the water.

Making tears
Crocodile tears are made in little sacs, and run onto the surface of the eye through tiny tubes. A special third eyelid smears the tears over the surface.

Grab a bite
When a crocodile snaps its jaws shut, the force of the bite may cause tears to squeeze out.

? True or false?

1. Crocodiles cry when they are sad.

2. Saltwater crocodiles are the biggest and weepiest crocodiles.

3. Many animals have three eyelids.

See pages 134–135 for the answers

Answers

Page 8 1) Packs that hunt big elk can have 15–20 members. 2) Usually different packs stay away from each other. But if they meet up they may fight. 3) Wolves howl to bring members of the pack together and to scare off other packs. **Page 11** 1) Having an appearance that helps an animal to blend into its surroundings. 2) Not many other cats have stripes. The European wild cat has stripy markings, as do some pet cats. 3) Their stripes may dazzle and confuse predators, or help individuals recognise one another. **Page 12** 1) Yes, bats have good vision. However, like many mammals active at night, most cannot see colour. 2) Most bats use their voice box, but a few can click with their tongues. Some bats have fleshy structures on their nose that work like megaphones. 3) No, some bats eat fruit, nectar, or pollen. Some big bats eat birds, lizards, frogs, or even fish. And vampire bats have a taste for blood. **Page 15** 1) The Arctic. 2) They have a layer of fat, called blubber, which helps keep body warmth trapped inside. 3) Males sometimes use their tusks for fighting. **Page 17** A swan. **Page 19** A placental. **Page 21** 1) Africa and tropical Asia. 2) Elephants can probably live up to about 70 years. 3) The oldest female – and leader – of an elephant herd. **Page 23** 1) False. Some water is produced when a camel burns the fat in its hump, but it relies on drinking water. 2) True. Camels were introduced to Australia by humans. 3) True. The spit is also mixed with some spewed-up stomach contents for extra effect! **Page 24** A husky. **Page 27** 1) No, only spider monkeys, woolly monkeys, and howler monkeys have prehensile tails. 2) Gibbons can reach top speeds of 55 kph (34 mph). They are actually

small apes, rather than monkeys. 3) Many monkeys have opposable thumbs and big toes, meaning that they can grasp around a branch with the opposite fingers and toes. **Page 29** A rat. Rat teeth grow continuously as they are worn down by chewing. **Page 30** 1) A lone sentry calls out with a shrieking bark. Everyone in the group then runs for safety. 2) They escape down burrows, which is also where they raise their young and sleep at night. 3) No, a group usually has 10–15 individuals from two or three families. **Page 32** 1) Their soft fur is like velvet and can lie flat in every direction. This helps a mole to easily move forwards and backwards through its burrow. 2) These are mounds of earth that are formed on the surface when moles push soil out of a deep tunnel. 3) A mole can eat half its body weight in food each day – mainly earthworms and insects. Star-nosed moles eat shrimps and fish. **Page 34** 1) Animals that rely on vision in bright daylight often have good colour vision. 2) Some people are born colour-blind because their eyes don't have all the working colour sensors for full colour vision. **Page 36** 1) They eat a wide range of different foods, including animals and plants. 2) Polar bear. 3) Giant panda. **Page 39** 1) The only land predators in Antarctica are seabirds. Penguin eggs and chicks could be eaten by seabirds, such as skuas and petrels. 2) Galápagos penguin. It is found only on the Galápagos Islands off the Pacific coast of South America, just south of the Equator. 3) No. There are plenty of land predators in the Arctic, such as the polar bear and Arctic fox, so birds need to be able to fly to escape danger. **Page 42** Kingfisher. **Page 44** 1) In zoos they don't have access to brine shrimps or algae, so they are

fed a special diet that contains the substance that makes them pink. 2) A baby flamingo is born with a straight beak. It becomes curved as it grows older. 3) One. **Page 46** 1) b. 2) a. An owl's eyes are so big that its eyeballs cannot move around. Owls have to turn their whole head to look in different directions. **Page 48** 1) False. This myth may have started because ostriches sometimes try to avoid danger by sitting down with their head and neck stretched out on the ground in front of them. 2) True. Ostriches can keep up a speed of 50 kph (30 mph) for half an hour – and can reach a top speed of 70 kph (40 mph). **Page 50** 1) b. 2) a. **Page 53** 1) Many birds that don't migrate feed mainly on things such as berries, seeds, or worms that are available all year round. Or they live in the tropics where it is always warm. 2) No, migrations follow many different kinds of routes depending on the needs of the animals. 3) No, long-distance migration can even happen on a daily basis. In the ocean many animals swim from the depths upwards to feed at the surface at night. **Page 54** Common swift. **Page 56** 1) Some hummingbirds build thimble-sized nests from cobwebs. Their eggs are no bigger than peas. 2) No, many seabirds lay their eggs on bare rocky ledges. The white tern lays its egg in a groove in a branch of a tree. 3) Many small mammals, stickleback fish, and crocodiles build nests for their young. Some insects, such as termites, build some of the biggest nests of any animal. **Page 58** 1) True. Adult emperor penguins can stand up to 130 cm (50 in) tall and are the fifth heaviest of all birds. 2) False. Other birds breed on the coastline, but no bird breeds as far south as the emperor penguin. **Page 61** 1) b. 2) c. A pair of eagles use

the same nest, built from sticks, each year, and keep adding to it so it gets bigger. **Page 63** 1) True. 2) True. For instance, they may do it to show off their territory. 3) True. **Page 66** 1) True. Many kinds of deep sea fish produce light – either for attracting mates, confusing predators, or luring in prey. 2) True. No rabbits can produce light naturally, but scientists have managed to make rabbits glow. **Page 69** 1) No, some kinds of parrotfish rely on finding a sheltered spot. 2) No, many fish are active at night and sleep during the day. **Page 70** 1) Yes, the biggest pufferfish use their teeth to open mussels, clams, and shellfish. 2) Tiny pufferfish can also puff up, but they usually rely on staying hidden among rocks to stay safe. 3) It slowly lets the seawater back out of its mouth. **Page 72** The flying squid. **Page 74** 1) False. Sharks that do bite humans generally do it by mistake. 2) True. They produce new teeth to replace the old ones that fall out. **Page 76** 1) Each coral polyp has tiny stingers on its tentacles. 2) Coral grows best in warm sun-lit waters. As a coral colony grows it forms huge, rocky outgrowths and the whole structure is called a reef. **Page 78** 1) a. 2) b. **Page 80** 1) The strange, tadpole-shaped snailfish could live the deepest. It lives at least 8,000 m (26,000 ft) below the surface. 2) Scientists can visit the deep sea in special submarine-like vehicles called submersibles. **Page 82** 1) Anemones eat tiny animals floating in the sea. Their stinging tentacles paralyse their prey. 2) Yes, all fish have a coating of slime. It helps protect them from parasites and injury. 3) Yes, anemones are animals that are related to jellyfish. **Page 85** The sidewinder, a type of rattlesnake. **Page 86** 1) True.

There are dozens of members of the piranha family and they all live in tropical South America. 2) False. Some piranhas eat seeds, nuts, or fruit. 3) False. They are most active during the day. **Page 89** 1) b. We only know about the spade-toothed whale because of a few individuals that have washed up on beaches. It has never been seen alive. 2) a. Whaling for profit was banned in 1986 to help whale populations recover. **Page 93** 1) A fly doesn't have the special waxy hairs that stop pond-skaters getting wet, so it gets trapped in the water. 2) An animal needs to be lightweight for the surface "skin" of water to support its body. 3) Yes. Some insects and spiders can. The tiny pygmy gecko, a type of lizard, has special water-repelling skin and is probably the smallest backboned animal that can walk on water. **Page 94** 1) False. Male honeybees are called drones and they stay near the hive. 2) False. Some kinds of bees, such as bumblebees, hibernate in the winter, but honeybees stay busy in the winter months. 3) True. Sugar-rich nectar is used to make honey. This provides the bees with energy. Pollen contains lots of protein and is needed to help the eggs grow into new bees. **Page 97** 1) There are other kinds of insects that feed on dung, but they don't bury it. If there were no dung beetles there would be more piles of dung on show! 2) Their legs are edged with special "teeth" – a bit like a garden rake. This helps them make the dung into a ball. 3) Mums of some kinds of dung beetles stay with the baby once it has hatched from its egg, in order to keep it clean. **Page 99** 1) No, the queen produces a chemical perfume that stops all her workers from breeding and laying eggs of their own. 2) Winged queens and drones (male ants) emerge

from the nest about once a year – usually during warm, humid weather. They do so to mate and produce new colonies. 3) No, there are more than 10,000 different species of ants, and they vary a lot in their behaviour. Army ants are aggressive meat-eaters that eat small animals. **Page 101** 1) False. Once a baby louse hatches, the empty egg turns white. These empty cases are called "nits". 2) False. Lice seem to have no preference between clean hair and dirty hair. 3) True. They can crawl out of one person's hair and into another's if the heads touch. **Page 103** 1) Yes, some spiders spin silken cocoons to lay their eggs in. Other tiny spiders fire a silk thread into the air and wait for it to be caught by the wind, carrying them with it. 2) The Darwin's bark spider from Madagascar can spin webs up to 25 m (82 ft) long. They can even stretch over rivers! 3) Complicated webs made from many sheets of silk that build up in size over time. **Page 104** 1) True. Because slugs do not have the protection of a shell, many prefer to stay sheltered underground or beneath logs. 2) True. Garden snails eat the leaves of plants. 3) True. Some kinds of snails live in the sea and most of those breathe using gills. **Page 107** 1) No, only female mosquitoes drink blood. Male mosquitoes feed on nectar from flowers. 2) Yes, in some countries certain kinds of mosquitoes spread dangerous diseases, such as malaria and yellow fever. 3) When a mosquito bites, it injects a chemical that helps the blood flow freely. Our body reacts to this chemical, making the bite feel itchy. **Page 108** The female Queen Alexandra's birdwing, a type of butterfly, has a wingspan of up to 28 cm (11 in). Two moths, the Atlas moth and the white witch, have wings about the same size.

Page 111 1) Some big tarantulas can producing a hissing sound by rubbing the bristles on their legs. Some snakes can make a sound by rubbing the scales of their skin together. 2) No, different kinds of grasshoppers produce different chirping sounds. 3) The cicada, a type of bug, has a buzzing song that is possibly the loudest sound made by any insect. **Page 115** 1) Geckos climb to reach their prey, such as insects. 2) No, some geckos live in habitats where climbing is not useful, such as in deserts. 3) The name comes from the chirping call of some kinds of gecko, which sounds like they are saying "gecko". **Page 117** 1) No, most relaxed chameleons are green or brown to blend in with their surroundings and only change colour when they get excited. 2) Some other kinds of lizards use crystals to change colour in the same way as chameleons. **Page 118** 1) Apart from a few kinds that eat eggs, all snakes kill living, moving prey. 2) Yes, rattlesnakes and some vipers have special sensors that can detect the body heat coming from warm-blooded prey. **Page 120** 1) Yes. 2) Wild axolotls are threatened with extinction, mainly due to the effects of pollution. **Page 122** The bombardier beetle. **Page 124** 1) False. Some kinds of poison dart frogs are more dangerous than others. 2) True. They can lose their poison in captivity when they are not fed the specific insects that are responsible for making them poisonous. **Page 127** Albatrosses. **Page 128** 1) Yes, the most northerly reptile is the viviparous lizard, which even reaches inside the Arctic Circle. 2) Most stay close to the warm surface in tropical regions. However, leatherback turtles can produce heat in their muscles, which helps them to live in colder parts of the

ocean. 3) Most animals, including amphibians, fish, and insects, are "cold-blooded". Birds and mammals (including us) are "warm-blooded". **Page 130** 1) Snakes and lizards have hard, dry scales that protect their skin, instead of slime. 2) Yes, the slime produced by humans is called mucus. When we sneeze it comes out as snot! 3) No, slime is sticky, so the entire surface of the frog stays protected by it, even when it swims in water. **Page 133** 1) False. 2) True. The saltwater crocodile is the only kind of crocodile that regularly swims out into salty sea water. It gets rid of some of the extra salt in its tears. 3) True. Some animals, including crocodiles, have third eyelids. They blink across the eyes to protect them and to help spread moisture.

Questions

1. Which bird has the **biggest bill** in relation to its body size?

2. Do centipedes really have 100 legs?

3. Which animal produces **square poo?**

4. How do rattlesnakes rattle?

5. Which bird can **fly backwards?**

6. Apart from humans, which other animal **sleeps on a mattress?**

7. How many **hearts** does an **octopus** have?

8. Can all cats purr?

9. Which animal lays the **biggest eggs?**

10. The **fathers** of which animal get **pregnant?**

Quiz your friends!

Who knows the most about the animal world? Test your friends and family with these tricky questions.

Answers

1. Toucan

2. They have **30 to 382 legs**, depending upon species – but none has exactly 100 legs.

3. Wombat

4. Their tail has extra-fast muscles for shaking hollow, rattling scales at its tip.

5. Hummingbird

6. Orang-utan. It builds a soft sleeping platform from leaves and twigs.

7. Three. Two are for pumping blood through the gills, and the third pumps blood to the other organs.

8. Big cats – tigers, lions, jaguars, and leopards – cannot purr, but roar instead.

9. Ostrich

10. A seahorse father collects fertilized eggs into his pouch so they can grow there until he **"gives birth"**.

Glossary

Algae
plant-like living things. Many are tiny and live in water

Amphibian
back-boned, cold-blooded animal with moist skin. Frogs, newts, and salamanders are amphibians. Most live on land, but breed in water

Antennae
"feelers" on the heads of certain kinds of creepy-crawlies

Camouflage
the way the appearance of an animal, such as its colour or shape, helps it to blend in with its surroundings

Carbon dioxide
gas that animals produce as a waste product. Animals get rid of carbon dioxide by breathing it out using lungs or gills

Carnivore
meat-eating animal

Cell
tiny unit that is the basic building block of all living things

Cold-blooded
reptiles, amphibians, fish, and creepy-crawlies are described as cold-blooded. This is because their body temperature varies, from cold to warm, with the temperature of their surroundings

Coral
animal that lives in a large group, called a colony, attached to the bottom of oceans or seas

Digestion
the way the body of an animal breaks down food so it can be carried to the body's cells

Echolocation
process of directing sounds at objects and listening for the echo that bounces back. Dolphins use echolocation to hunt fish in murky water. Bats use it to track flying insects at night

Endangered
when there are so few of an animal left in the wild that it is in danger of dying out altogether

Extinct
when there are no living members of a kind of animal left. For example, dinosaurs are extinct

Gill
part of the body used by some animals, such as fish, to breathe underwater. Oxygen in the water moves into the blood in the gills

Gland
part of the body that produces substances that are useful to the animal – such as sweat for cooling the skin, or spit for helping to digest food

Habitat
where an animal or plant normally lives

Herbivore
plant-eating animal

Hibernation
process where animals shut down their body systems and go into a deep sleep-state over winter. Hibernation is a useful way of surviving when temperatures drop and there isn't much food available

Invertebrate
an animal without a backbone. Creepy-crawlies are all invertebrates

Mammal
back-boned, warm-blooded animal, usually with furry skin. Humans, lions, and whales are all examples of mammals. Mothers of all mammals feed their young with milk

Marsupial
mammal that gives birth to especially tiny young, which are usually kept in a mother's pouch during the early stages of growth. Kangaroos and koalas are examples of marsupials

Migration
when animals travel between different places at regular intervals. This is usually to reach feeding or breeding grounds

Monotreme
mammal that lays eggs. The platypus and echidna are the only two kinds of monotremes

Muscle
part of the body that contracts (shortens) to cause movement. Some muscles are part of organs – such as the heart. Others are attached to the skeleton

Nerve
fibre in the body that carries electrical signals. Some nerves carry signals to the brain. Others carry signals to muscles to make them contract

Nocturnal
an animal that is active at night and sleeps during the day

Omnivore
an animal that eats both plants and animals

Organ
part of the body that performs a particular job. For instance, the heart is an organ for pumping blood

Oxygen
gas needed to support life. Animals get oxygen by breathing it in using lungs, gills, or their skin

Paralyse
animals are paralysed when their muscles stop working, so they cannot move. Some animals produce a venom that paralyses their prey

Pheromone
chemical scent released by an animal to signal a message to other animals of the same kind. For example, to warn others of danger

Placental
type of mammal that keeps babies in its womb so they can grow bigger before they are born. Placentals include humans, mice, and elephants

Plankton
tiny animals and plants that swim or float in the water of the sea or a pond. Some can only be seen clearly with a microscope

Polyp
living creature that joins with many others of its kind to form a coral reef. Each polyp has stinging tentacles for grabbing prey

Predator
animal that kills another living thing for food

Prey
animal that is killed by a predator and used as food

Queen
egg-laying female in a colony of certain types of insects, such as bees, ants, or termites

Reef
large rocky structure, usually around tropical coastlines, formed by the growth of coral

Reptile
back-boned, cold-blooded animal with dry, scaly skin. Turtles, lizards, snakes, and crocodiles are reptiles and most lay eggs on land

Sea anemone
soft-bodied animal in oceans and seas that has stinging tentacles to catch small animals

Scavenger
animal that gets its food by eating the leftovers of other animals

Tusk
long tooth, which often extends out of the mouth. Elephants and walruses have tusks

Ultraviolet
type of light that can only be seen by certain kinds of animals – for example, bees. Humans cannot see ultraviolet light

Venom
chemical that a biting or stinging animal uses for hunting or defence

Vertebrate
animals with a backbone. Fish, amphibians, reptiles, birds, and mammals are vertebrates

Warm-blooded
mammals and birds are described as warm-blooded. This is because their body produces enough heat to keep them warm, even when the surroundings are cold

Index

Acknowledgements

DORLING KINDERSLEY would like to thank: Caroline Hunt for proofreading and Helen Peters for the index.

The publisher would like to thank the following for their kind permission to reproduce their photographs:

(Key: a-above; b-below/bottom; c-centre; f-far; l-left; r-right; t-top)

4 Dreamstime.com: Shawn Hempel (crb). **8-9 Alamy Images:** Corbis Super RF (t). **9 Alamy Images:** Matthias Graben / imageBROKER (bl); Duncan Murrell / Steve Bloom Images (bc). **10 Corbis:** Peter Langer / Design Pics (bl); Norbert Wu / Minden Pictures (cl). **10-11 Dreamstime.com:** Julian W / julianwphoto. **12-13 Corbis:** Michael Durham / Minden Pictures (t). **13 Alamy Images:** FLPA (bc). **Getty Images:** Alexander Safonov / Barcroft Media (bl). **14-15 Corbis:** Sergey Gorshkov / Minden Pictures. **14 Getty Images:** Paul Nicklen / National Geographic (bl); Manoj Shah / Oxford Scientific (clb). **16-17 Alamy Images:** Martin Harvey. **17 Alamy Images:** Andrew Parkinson (tr). **Getty Images:** Nick Garbutt / Barcroft Media (br); MyLoupe / UIG (cr). **18-19 Corbis:** David Watts / Visuals Unlimited. **18 Dorling Kindersley:** Booth Museum of Natural History, Brighton (cb). **19 Alamy Images:** Fixed Focus (tl). **20-21 Alamy Images:** Johan Swanepoel. **21 Dreamstime.com:** Stephenmeese (tl). **FLPA:** Michael & Patricia Fogden / Minden Pictures (tc). **22 Corbis:** Karl Van Ginderdeuren / Buiten-beeld (bl). **Fotolia:** Peter Wey (clb). **22-23 Dreamstime.com:** Yuriy Zelenen'kyy / Zrelenenkyyyuriy. **24 Corbis:** David Cavagnaro / Visuals Unlimited (tr). **24-25 Getty Images:** J. Sneesby / B. Wilkins / The Image Bank. **25 Corbis:** Tom Brakefield (tl); Mark Payne-Gill / Nature Picture Library (tc). **26-27 Alamy Images:** FLPA. **27 Alamy Images:** Frans Lanting Studio (br). **Getty Images:** Sandra Leidholdt / Moment Open (bc). **28-29 Getty Images:** Don Baird. **29 Alamy Images:** Nigel Cattlin (br). **Corbis:** Mike Parry / Minden Pictures (tr). **Dorling Kindersley:** Thomas Marent (cr). **30-31 Alamy Images:** kristianbell / RooM The Agency. **31 Getty Images:** Sylvain Oliveira (crb). **Getty Images:** Adegsm (t). **32 Alamy Images:** blickwinkel / Hartl (bl). **FLPA:** Michael & Patricia Fogden / Minden Pictures (cl). **32-33 Corbis:** Ken Catania / Visuals Unlimited. **34-35 Dreamstime.com:** Pressureua (b). **35 Corbis:** Joseph Giacomin / cultura (tc). **Dreamstime.com:** Studioloco (br). **Science Photo Library:** Cordelia Molloy (tl). **36 Getty Images:** Jonathan Kantor / Stone (tl). **36-37 Dreamstime.com:** Petr Mašek / Petrmasek. **37 Dreamstime.com:** Emilia Stasiak (tc). **Getty Images:** Antony Dickson / AFP (tl). **38 Corbis:** Alaska Stock. **39 Corbis:** W. Perry Conway (tr). **Getty Images:** Hakan Karlsson (cr). **42 Alamy Images:** Naturfoto-Online (bl). **Corbis:** Dale Spartas (c). **42-43 Dreamstime.com:** Pavlo Kucherov (b). **iStockphoto.com:** GlobalP. **43 Dreamstime.com:** Kim Worrell (crb). **Getty Images:** Stephen Frink (br). **44-45 Dreamstime.com:** Mikhail Matsonashvili (Water). **Getty Images:** Gerry Ellis / Digital Vision (b). **45 Dreamstime.com:** Orlandin (br). **Rex Shutterstock:** Mohamed Babu / Solent News (crb). **46-47 Corbis:** Christian Naumann / dpa. **47 123RF.com:** dipressionist (bc); Michael Lane (bl). **48 naturepl.com:** Klein & Hubert (c). **48-49 naturepl.com:** Klein & Hubert (b). **49 Alamy Images:** The Natural History Museum (c). **Corbis:** Stephen Belcher / Minden Pictures (crb). **naturepl.com:** Klein & Hubert (c). **50-51 Dreamstime.com:** Shawn Hempel (c). **51 Dreamstime.com:** Iakov Filimonov (br/pheasant); Alexander Potapov (br). **naturepl.com:** Andy Rouse (tr). **52-53 Alamy Images:** Arco Images / de Cuveland, J. (c). **53 Alamy Images:** FLPA (tc). **Dreamstime.com:** Gillian Hardy (tr). **Getty Images:** Mint Images / Art Wolfe (cr); Wayne Lynch (tc/arctic tern chick). **54-55 Dreamstime.com:** Sim Kay Seng (c). **54 Corbis:** Mike Danzenbaker / BIA / Minden Pictures (cl). **55 Getty Images:** Tom Robinson (br). **56-57 Getty Images:** Visuals Unlimited, Inc. / Joe McDonald. **57 Alamy Images:** Werli Francois (bl). **Dreamstime.com:** Linkman (cra). **Getty Images:** Visuals Unlimited, Inc. / Dave Watts (crb). **58-59 Getty Images:** Johnny Johnson (c). **59 Alamy Images:** Thomas Kitchin & Victoria Hurst / Design Pics Inc (tc). **Corbis:** Frank Lukasseck (br). **FLPA:** Flip Nicklin (tl). **60-61 naturepl.com:** Inaki Relanzon (c). **60 123RF.com:** andreanita (bl). **Getty Images:** Ed George (bc). **62 Corbis:** Tui De Roy / Minden Pictures (clb). **Getty Images:** David Haring / DUPC (bl). **62-63 Alamy Images:** Christine Barraclough (c). **66-67 Photoshot:** Biosphoto. **67 Alamy Images:** blickwinkel / Hauke (br). **naturepl.com:** Solvin Zankl (crb). **68-69 Alamy Images:** Reinhard Dirscherl. **68 Alamy Images:** Norbert Schuster / Premium Stock Photography GmbH (bc). **Dreamstime.com:** Sergey Skleznev (bl). **70-71 Corbis:** Visuals Unlimited (b). **Dreamstime.com:** Irochka (Background). **70 Dreamstime.com:** Marco Lijoi (clb). **71 123RF.com:** Norman Krau (br). **Getty Images:** Ian West (cr). **72-73 Dreamstime.com:** Felix Renaud (b). **Getty Images:** Sylvain Cordier (cb). **naturepl.com:** Brent Stephenson (c). **72 Alamy Images:** Anthony Pierce / robertharding (bl). **73 Corbis:** Stephen Dalton / Minden Pictures (bc); Joe McDonald (bl). **74-75 Getty Images:** Michele Westmorland (t). **75 123RF.com:** Yutakapong Chuynugul (cr); Marc Henauer (bc). **Corbis:** Jeffrey L. Rotman (cb). **iStockphoto.com:** lilithlita (tr). **76-77 Alamy Images:** Reinhard Dirscherl (b). **Dreamstime.com:** Vdevolder (Background). **77 Dreamstime.com:** Serg_dibrova (crb); Mychadre77 (br). **naturepl.com:** Roberto Rinaldi (cla). **78-79 Ardea:** Augusto Leandro Stanzani (c). **79 Alamy Images:** Marshall Ikonography (cr). **Getty Images:** Gerhard Schulz (br). **80 naturepl.com:** David Shale (clb, cb). **80-81 Corbis:** David Shale / Nature Picture Library (bc). **81 Getty Images:** Norbert Wu (b). **Science Photo Library:** Richard R. Hansen (tl); Vincent Amouroux , Mona Lisa Production (tc). **82 Fotolia:** uwimages (c). **82-83 Dreamstime.com:** Irochka (Background). **iStockphoto.com:** strmko

(c). **83 Corbis:** Dray van Beeck / NiS / Minden Pictures (br). **Dreamstime.com:** Camptoloma (tc); Lightdreams (c). **Fotolia:** uwimages (cb). **iStockphoto.com:** Dovapi (cr). **Photoshot:** Daniel Heuclin / NHPA (tl). **84 Alamy Images:** donna Ikenberry / Art Directors (bl). **Corbis:** Hal Beral (clb). **84-85 Alamy Images:** Teila K. Day Photography (c). **85 Photoshot:** (tr). **86-87 Dreamstime.com:** Goce Risteski (c). **86 Alamy Images:** Heather Angel / Natural Visions (bc). **Corbis:** Michael & Patricia Fogden (bl). **87 Dreamstime.com:** Mikhailsh. **88 Science Photo Library:** Alexis Rosenfeld. **89 Dreamstime.com:** Johannes Gerhardus Swanepoel (bl); Bidouze Stéphane (bc). **92-93 Alamy Images:** blickwinkel. **93 Alamy Images:** David Chapman (ca). **Corbis:** Stephen Dalton / Nature Picture Library (tc). **94-95 Robert Harding Picture Library:** Michael Weber (c). **95 naturepl.com:** Tim Laman / National Geographic Creative (br). **Rex Shutterstock:** Jurgen Otto / Solent News (cr). **96-97 Corbis:** Mitsuhiko Imamori / Minden Pictures. **96 Alamy Images:** Kari Niemeläinen (bl); Paul R. Sterry / Nature Photographers Ltd (clb). **97 Dreamstime.com:** Sakdinon Kadchiangsaen / Sakdinon (tr). **98-99 Alamy Images:** Kim Taylor / Nature Picture Library. **99 Alamy Images:** Frans Lanting Studio (bc); GFC Collection (bl). **100 Alamy Images:** David Hosking (bc). **Science Photo Library:** Power And Syred (bl). **100-101 Science Photo Library:** Steve Gschmeissner (c). **102-103 Corbis:** Hannie Joziasse / Buiten-beeld / Minden Pictures (bc). **102 Corbis:** Dennis Kunkel Microscopy, Inc. / Visuals Unlimited (bc). **103 Corbis:** Stephen Dalton / Minden Pictures (cr); Seraf van der Putten / Buiten-beeld / Minden Pictures (br). **104-105 Alamy Images:** blickwinkel / Teigler (c). **105 Alamy Images:** Carlos Villoch / VWpics / Visual&Written SL (cr). **Corbis:** Martin Harvey (br). **106-107 Getty Images:** Media for Medical / Universal Images Group (c). **106 Getty Images:** Tim Flach / Stone (c). **107 Alamy Images:** blickwinkel / Hecker (bc). **Corbis:** Rene Krekels / NiS / Minden Pictures (br). **108 Alamy Images:** The Natural History Museum, London (b). **Dorling Kindersley:** Natural History Museum, London (tl). **Getty Images:** Tim Flach / Stone (tr); Gerard Lacz / Visuals Unlimited, Inc. (cl). **109 Corbis:** Mark Moffett / Minden Pictures (t). **110-111 naturepl.com:** Kim Taylor (c). **110 Corbis:** Michael & Patricia Fogden (bl); Hiroya Minakuchi / Minden Pictures (cl). **114 Science Photo Library:** Power And Syred (c). **114-115 4Corners:** Andrea Vecchiato / SIME. **115 123RF.com:** rclassenlayouts (cr). **Corbis:** HAGENMULLER Jean-Francois / Hemis (br). **116-117 Getty Images:** MarkBridger (c). **117 Alamy Images:** aroona kavathekar (bc/beetle). **Dreamstime.com:** Xunbin Pan (bc). **naturepl.com:** John Downer Productions (bl). **118 Corbis:** Ivan Kuzmin / imageBROKER (c). **119 123RF.com:** happystock (tc). **iStockphoto.com:** bucky_za (tl); CathyKeifer (tr). **120-121 Dreamstime.com:** Vdevolder (Background). **naturepl.com:** Jane Burton (c). **121 Alamy Images:** Images&Stories (crb). **iStockphoto.com:** AlasdairJames (br). **122 naturepl.com:** Nature Production (cl). **122-123 Corbis:** Patrick Kientz / Copyright : www. biosphoto.com / Biosphoto (c). **123 Corbis:** John Downer / Nature Picture Library (cr). **124-125 Dorling Kindersley:** Thomas Marent (c). **125 Corbis:** Thomas Marent / Minden Pictures (cr). **Dreamstime.com:** Pascal Halder (tr). **Science Photo Library:** Eye Of Science (bc). **126-127 Dreamstime.com:** Marcin Ciesielski / Sylwia Cisek / Eleaner (c). **126 Corbis:** Mitsuhiko Imamori / Minden Pictures (bc); Flip Nicklin / Minden Pictures (bl). **127 Corbis:** Frans Lanting (tr). **128 Alamy Images:** Oleksandr Lysenko (bl); Ryan M. Bolton (cl). **128-129 Alamy Images:** Maresa Pryor / Danita Delimont, Agent (c). **129 NASA:** JPL (cra). **130-131 Getty Images:** The Asahi Shimbun (c). **131 Alamy Images:** Mark Conlin (br); Ernie Janes (bc). **Corbis:** Michael & Patricia Fogden (tr). **naturepl.com:** Brandon Cole (crb). **132-133 Getty Images:** Danita Delimont / Gallo Images (c). **132 Alamy Images:** Sohns / imageBROKER (bl). **Getty Images:** MOF / Vetta (bc). **133 Corbis:** Martin Harvey (tc). **137 Dorling Kindersley:** Jerry Young (tr). **Dreamstime.com:** Achmat Jappie (bl) **140 Dreamstime.com:** Vaeenma (bc). **141 Dorling Kindersley:** Greg and Yvonne Dean (bl). **142 naturepl.com:** Roberto Rinaldi (bc); **Fotolia:** uwimages (br). **143 Dorling Kindersley:** Twan Leenders (br). **145 Dorling Kindersley:** Twan Leenders (tr).

Jacket:
(Key: a-above; b-below/bottom; c-centre; f-far; l-left; r-right; t-top)

Jacket images: Front: **Dorling Kindersley:** Greg and Yvonne Dean tr, Thomas Marent ca/ (Strawberry Poison Dart Frog), Natural History Museum, London tc; **Dreamstime.com:** Cynoclub fcla, Achmat Jappie bc, Vaeenma cra/ (cricket); **Fotolia:** uwimages cla; **Photolibrary:** White / Digital Zoo bl; Back: **Corbis:** Visuals Unlimited c; **Dorling Kindersley:** Jerry Young bl

All other images © Dorling Kindersley
For further information see: www.dkimages.com